KALAMKARI
TEMPLE HANGINGS

KALAMKARI TEMPLE HANGINGS

Anna L. Dallapiccola

Introduction by
Anna L. Dallapiccola and Rosemary Crill

Mapin Publishing in association with V&A Publishing, London

First published in India in 2015 by
Mapin Publishing
706 Kaivanna, Panchavati, Ellisbridge
Ahmedabad 380006 INDIA
T: +91 79 40228228 | F: +91 79 40228201
E: mapin@mapinpub.com | www.mapinpub.com

in association with
V&A Publishing
Victoria and Albert Museum
Cromwell Road
London SW7 2RL
T: 44 (0)20 7942 2966
www.vandapublishing.com

Simultaneously published in the
United States of America in 2015 by
Grantha Corporation
77 Daniele Drive, Hidden Meadows
Ocean Township, NJ 07712
E: mapin@mapinpub.com

Distribution
North America
ACC Distribution
6 West 18th Street, New York, NY 10011
T: +1 800 252 5231 | E: sales@antiquecc.com
www.accdistribution.com/us

United Kingdom, Europe, Austrailia & New Zealand
Littlehampton Book Services Ltd
Faraday Close, Durrington,
West Sussex BN13 3RB, UK
T: +44 (0) 1903 828501 | F: +44 (0) 1903 828801
E: customerservices@lbsltd.co.uk

Thailand, Laos, Cambodia, Myanmar
Paragon Asia Co. Ltd
Bangkok, Thailand
T: +66 2 877 7755 | E: info@paragonasia.com

Malaysia
Areca Books
Penang, Malaysia
T: +60 4 2610307 | E: arecabooks@gmail.com
www.arecabooks.com

Rest of the World
Mapin Publishing Pvt. Ltd

Text ©authors
Images ©Victoria and Albert Museum, London
except those listed below:
- Illustrations on pp. 11, 12, 69: Courtesy of the Trustees of the British Museum
- Photo on pp. 4–5: Dinodia Photo Library
- Photo on p. 16: Pushkar V.

All rights reserved under international copyright conventions. No part of this book may be reproduced or transmitted in any form or by any means, electronic or mechanical, including photocopy, recording or any other information storage and retrieval system, without prior permission in writing from the publisher.

ISBN: 978-93-85360-04-6 (Mapin)
ISBN: 978-1-935677-62-8 (Grantha)
ISBN: 978-1-85177-867-6 (V&A)
LCCN: 2015945259

Copyediting: Vinutha Mallya / Mapin Editorial
Editorial Assistance: Neha Manke / Mapin Editorial
Design: Gopal Limbad / Mapin Design Studio
Production Assistance: Rakesh Manger / Mapin Design Studio
Printed at Tien Wah Press, Malaysia

Page 1
Sri Krishnasvami kills Aghasura
(cat. 9, fig. 38, detail)

Pages 2–3
Sri Krishnasvami plays flute to the *gopikas*
(cat. 9, fig. 54, detail)

Pages 4–5
Golden dome above the main sanctuary,
Sri Ranganathasvami Temple, Srirangam

Contents

Introduction   9

The Ramayana: 'Constructed, Killed and Brought'   24

① Ramayana Chirala   26
② Ramayana Machilipatnam   43
③ Ramayana Srikalahasti   56
④ Ramayana Srikalahasti (English captions)   70
⑤ Ramayana Sri Lanka   78

    RAMAYANA: SELECTED SCENES   96
⑥ Balakanda Madurai   96
⑦ Yuddhakanda Madurai   103
⑧ Ramapattabhisheka Madurai   107

⑨ Krishnacharita Coastal Andhra   111

Two Episodes from the Mahabharata   123

⑩ The Killing of Shishupala Madurai   124
⑪ The Duel between Karna and Arjuna Madurai   128

Two Ganga Hangings   132

⑫ Ganga Duppati Machilipatnam   135
⑬ Ganga Duppati Machilipatnam   146

⑭ Mahalakshmi Pithakam Machilipatnam   156

Introduction to the Holy Sites   158

⑮ Sri Subrahmanya Temple, Tiruchendur   159
⑯ Sri Subrahmanyasvami Temple, Tirupparankunram   164
⑰ Sri Ranganathasvami Temple, Srirangam   170
⑱ Alagar Koyil Chittirai Festival   174
⑲ The Life of Christ Srikalahasti   179

Bibliography   187
Glossary   189
Acknowledgements   192

1. Mural in the *gopura*, Sri Narumpunata Temple, Tiruppudaimarudur

Introduction

A.L. Dallapiccola and Rosemary Crill

This book deals with a group of painted and dyed cloths from southern India, in the form of hangings and canopies, commissioned by Hindu temples and *maths* (monasteries), and by individuals for religious use. Other related hangings, made for the local market, were also created for secular use at local courts.[1] They were produced by a complicated process known as *kalamkari*, 'pen work', of which the main characteristic is hand-drawing of the design with a *kalam* (bamboo pen) and dyeing of the cloth, rather than printing or other surface applications of colour. European merchants had various names for this technique: the Portuguese called it *pintado*, the Dutch *sitz*, the British chintz, and today the designation '*kalamkari*' is widely used, although this has also come to include printed textiles made around Machilipatnam. How, when and where the *kalamkari* technique originated is not known: the oldest surviving examples date from the 15th–16th century and were made for export to South-East Asia, although the technique was undoubtedly already in use at an earlier date and for a much wider local and export market.[2]

Although textiles are often discussed in the early accounts of travellers, the South Indian temple cloths are not mentioned. They were first noticed outside India at the Colonial Exhibition of 1886 at South Kensington. On this occasion, the *Ramayana* from Srikalahasti (cat. 3) was acquired for the South Kensington Museum's collection.[3] The reasons for this neglect are twofold: first of all, the 17th- and 18th-century European traders were not in direct contact with the master dyers, but dealt almost exclusively with Indian merchants and factors, and probably had no opportunity of seeing temple cloths, which were made for local use rather than export. Furthermore, even if they had come across them, they would have considered their bold designs and vibrant colours crude and rough especially when compared to the delicacy of chintz made for the European market, which used finely drawn wax-resist and more complex dyeing methods to produce much more intricate patterns.

Unfortunately, on account of the fragile nature of the cotton on to which the paintings were executed, which is adversely affected by light, heat, and humidity, only very few fragments of temple cloths which may be datable to the 18th century have come down to us.[4] The majority of the cloths, which are now in public and private collections, were produced in the 19th and 20th centuries.

Temple hangings were used in various ways: as decoration behind, or in the case of a canopy, above an image, or to screen off spaces for particular ceremonies. Their most important function was didactic, as they were used as visual accompaniment to the recitation of episodes from the epics or from the *Puranas*. Their layout is strongly influenced by the local traditions of wall painting and, as observed by Irwin and Hall, "in some cases it would not be inaccurate to describe them as murals on cloth"[5] (see ill. 1). As is the case in South Indian murals, the narratives illustrated in the hangings are laid out in registers. Architectural forms, such as lobed arches and pillars, or trees and shrubs, are commonly used as framing devices, which help the decoding of the painted narrative. Frequently the scenes bear explanatory captions, and occasionally, individual characters are identified by a label.

THEMES

- **Epics and Puranas**

    Judging from the surviving material, the *Ramayana* seems to have been one of the most popular subjects, as demonstrated by the holdings of the Victoria and Albert Museum in which the majority of the temple cloths were inspired by it (cat.1–cat. 8). This is not surprising, as the story of Rama is comparatively easy to follow, and there is only one, undisputed hero: Rama. Extremely rare are hangings depicting a resumé of the whole *Mahabharata*. An example from Srikalahasti, a true *tour de force* on the part of the artist, dating from the first half of the 20th century, is now in the collection of the British Museum (see ill. 2).[6] In general, only a few key episodes of the *Mahabharata* are illustrated: the killing of Shishupala (cat. 10), the battle between Karna and Arjuna (cat. 11), the story of the wedding of Vatsala and Abhimanyu,[7] and the adventures of the five Pandava brothers and Draupadi at the court of King Virata.[8] Finally, the V&A collection has one very fine canopy illustrating the story of Krishna, inspired by the *Bhagavata Purana* narrative (cat. 9).

- **Holy places**

    Tamil Nadu is particularly rich in temples, most of them popular sites of pilgrimage. The depiction of holy places is an important theme which appears often in South Indian art, particularly from the 16th century onwards. Its popularity could be related to the emergence of provincial capitals as seats of power, as well as to the growth of pilgrimage centres within the Vijayanagara-ruled territory. Today, the so-called 'calendar prints' are a continuation of this age-revered tradition.

    Sacred sites in southern India are connected by a network of related deities, which determine the pilgrim's itinerary, e.g. the extremely popular visit to the six sites connected to the life of Subrahmanya (see cat. 15 and cat. 16). Particularly relevant

Introduction

among the Vaishnava sites are the Kallalagar temple at Alagar Koyil (see cat. 18), renowned, among others, for its connection to the Minakshi Sundareshvara Temple in nearby Madurai; the most famous of all the 108 Vaishnava *divyadeshams*, 'sacred abodes', is, however, the Sriranganatha Temple on Srirangam island (see ill. 3 and pp. 4–5; cat. 17).

2. Mahabharata from Srikalahasti, early 20th century, British Museum, Asia As1966,01.497

3. Plan of Sriranganatha Temple, Srirangam, Thanjavur, c. 1830, British Museum, Asia As1962,1231,0.13.1

- **Telugu epics**

  Among the hangings in the V&A's collection are two Ganga '*duppati*' (cat. 12 and cat. 13) whose narrative is inspired by the *Katamaraju Katha*, 'the story of Katamaraju', a narrative genealogy of the Gollas or Yadavas, the most important herding community of Andhra and Telangana. The hangings were used in the performance of the epic, the oldest and, possibly, longest cycle of ballads in the Telugu oral tradition of Andhra. The incidents displayed on these cloths focus on the exploits of Katamaraju, the main hero, deemed to be an incarnation of Krishna, and of his immediate predecessors. As far as we know, these are the only examples of Ganga '*duppati*' in UK public collections. Unfortunately, as the scholarship on the *Katamaraju Katha* is at an early stage, the available information on this fascinating and important work is very scarce and extremely difficult to obtain. There are problems with the reading of the inscriptions, the sequence of the episodes depicted, and the study of these cloths raises many questions which, for the time being, remain unanswered.[9]

- **Christian subjects**

  A more recent acquisition is the hanging depicting the 'Life of Christ' (cat. 19) by the master dyer Jonnagaladda Gurappa Chetty of Srikalahasti. This vibrant work prepared in 1981–82 for the Festival of India in London is an outstanding example of the revival of the Srikalahasti *kalamkari* craft in the last half-century. As demonstrated here, the artists expanded their repertoire exploring subjects outside their cultural tradition.

CENTRES OF PRODUCTION

"The outside is covered with a strong and coarse red cloth, ornamented with large variegated stripes; but the inside is lined with beautiful hand-painted chintz, manufactured for the purpose at *Maslipatam*, the ornamentation of which is set off by rich figured satin of various colours and embroideries of silk, silver, and gold, with deep and elegant fringes."[10] Particularly interesting in this description of the imperial tent written by François Bernier in c. 1657, is the mention of 'Maslipatam' (present-day Machilipatnam), which, along with Srikalahasti, was one of the major centres of South Indian *kalamkari* production. Apart from these two towns, other centres of production were Petaboli in the Krishna delta, St Thome[11] (present-day Chennai) and Nagapattinam. Yet another important centre of *kalamkari* production was in or near Madurai (see cat. 6–8, 10, 11, 15–18). However, although the production sites are known from historical documents, not one workshop can be linked with a surviving cloth dating prior to the late 19th century when some master dyers wrote on their cloth the place and the date where it was executed, as well as their own names.[12]

One of the few extensive surveys of *kalamkari* work is W.S. Hadaway's *Cotton Painting and Printing in the Madras Presidency* (Madras, 1917). In this, as well as

Machilipatnam, Madurai and Kalahasti, Hadaway mentions less well-known centres such as Sikkinayakanpet, Kumbakonam, Ponneri and Palakollu, where he remarks, "perhaps... the best temple cloths were made."[13] This echoes the remarks of E.B. Havell in his earlier article on the arts and crafts of Madras, in which he states: "At Pellacollu... there is one excellent workman whose hand-painted canopies and screens are equal to any made elsewhere. The best have mythological subjects similar to those of Kalahasti (which are better known)."[14] Hadaway also includes an extensive list of places where painted or printed cottons were being made in 1885–88, according to lists compiled by Havell.[15] While most of these places are listed as producing such goods as 'inferior turbans' or 'rough palampores', there is also a mention of 'painted cloths with mythological subjects' being made at Pennagudi, Salem.[16]

One of the pieces in the V&A collection (cat. 5) can be attributed to Sri Lanka, and was presumably made by Tamil craftsmen (the inscriptions are in Tamil) in the north of the island. The Sri Lankan production of temple cloths is even less well-documented than that of South India, although the manufacture of finer cloths in the chintz technique there is starting to be better understood.[17] Locally made banners and flags are also known, but these are mostly simple designs with animal emblems.[18] A notable exception that is clearly comparable to the V&A's *Ramayana* hanging (cat. 5) is illustrated by E.W. Perera[19] and is described as a '*Ramayana* war *kodiya*' (flag) from a temple in Kandy. It shows the speckled background and narrative registers also seen on the V&A piece.[20]

- **Machilipatnam**
The Machilipatnam master dyers prepared canopies with the appropriate mythological designs for their Hindu clients, prayer carpets for the Muslims, tent-lining cloths with cypress-motif or floral designs, which were held in high esteem by the Persian rulers, and finally, yardage and hangings of chintz for the Western market. The town was also an important trading centre from which the products of all the neighbouring area would be sold, for export as well as the home market, so pieces recorded as coming from Machilipatnam were not necessarily made there. The printing-and-dyeing industry flourished there until about the middle of the 19th century, with the Iranian trade continuing after trade with the West had declined in the wake of the prohibitions of 1701 and 1721. The great cyclone of 1864 also dealt the Machilipatnam textile production and trade a severe blow. At the beginning of the 20th century, *The Imperial Gazetteer of India, Provincial Series–Madras* (1908) notes: "An Industry for which Southern India was celebrated was the manufacture of block printed and hand-printed cotton stuffs. Its decline was rendered conspicuous by a comparison of the collection of these fabrics exhibited at the Delhi Darbar Exhibition in 1903 with the splendid series which was sent to the colonial Exhibition at London in 1886 [which included cat. 3]. Now-a-days

at former centres of this industry e.g. Masulipatam and Walajapet, old wood-blocks, many with elaborate and beautiful patterns of Persian origin, may be seen piled up in corners or in the roof covered with dust and cobwebs of years…"[21] By the 1950s there were practically no craftsmen left, but eventually the craft was gradually revived, thanks to the efforts of Kamaladevi Chattopadhyaya and the formation of the All India Handicrafts Board.

- **Srikalahasti**

Srikalahasti, formerly Kalahasti, is a temple town situated about 40 kilometres east of Tirupati. The town is ideally located on the bank of the River Svarnamukhi, which provides a constant supply of fresh running water, one of the most important elements of the *kalamkari* production process. It is probable that Srikalahasti was at the centre of the production and trade of *kalamkaris* since the 15th or 16th century, but firm evidence for their manufacture there, either through surviving pieces or written records, only dates from the 19th century. The religious importance of the place and the patronage of the local *zamindars* undoubtedly contributed to the development of the industry. The production of a temple cloth is expensive as it involves considerable labour and the demand for such works is limited. Only a few families were engaged in the preparation of temple cloths and, when in the 1930s and 1940s the commissions slowly dwindled, the craft died out almost completely. Interestingly, the craftsmen seemed to have been aware of this and prepared themselves to find other means of livelihood.[22] Thus, for example, Jonnalagadda Lakshmaiah, the then oldest surviving *kalamkari* artist, was a trained teacher. His own son, Jonnalagadda Gurappa Chetty, although an accomplished artist, was also a teacher. He, however, returned to his original vocation and became one of the most famous *kalamkari* artists (see cat. 19) who was awarded the prestigious Padma Shri, by Government of India. His son is continuing the family tradition.

The production of temple cloths was revived by the All India Handicrafts Board, under whose auspices a pilot production-cum-training centre was organized at Panagal, on the outskirts of Srikalahasti in 1958. Jonnalagadda Lakshmaiah was appointed as an instructor, and thus he was in the position to pass his knowledge to the younger generation. The repertoire of the Srikalahasti master dyers has now expanded to include, among others, Biblical stories, as in cat. 19.

- **Madurai**

Hand-painted cloths with mythological subjects are mentioned as being made at Madurai in E.B. Havell's survey of the cotton-painting industry published in 1889.[23] Havell remarks that Madura [Madurai] is famous for a fine red dye of a deep red colour, which is also produced in other places but that of Madura is superior in colour and fastness. This is attributed locally to the particular properties of the water of the River

Vaigai which runs through the city.[24] George Birdwood, in *The Industrial Arts of India*, states that "At Madura, large quantities of the stained cloth for which it is celebrated are manufactured. They are very coarse and printed [*sic*] in only two colours, red and black, with mythological subjects taken from the *Ramayana* and the *Mahabharata*. They are made chiefly for the service of the temples, and are very rare to get, except by favour of the priests".[25] The description corresponds with catalogue numbers 6–8, 10–11 and 15–18 in the present volume.

The technique of temple cloths

The hangings described in this book can all be categorised as belonging to the *kalamkari* tradition: that is, they all use predominantly hand-drawn outlines rather than printed ones and they all use dyeing techniques for their colours rather than surface application of pigments. This separates them from the other categories of textiles that have coloured designs and hand-drawing, especially the *pichhwai* of Rajasthan which use surface-applied colours rather than those produced by immersion in dye vats. The use of hand-drawing, with a simple bamboo-and-string tool called a *kalam* ('pen', from the Arabic word for reed, see ill. 4) also sets them clearly apart from textiles patterned exclusively by block-printing, such as the early Gujarati fragments found in Egypt.

The hangings fall into several styles of drawing, coloration and quality, and yet they share several basic technical characteristics: the use of cotton as their ground fabric; the use of hand-drawing with a *kalam*; the use of resist-dyeing and of mordant-dyeing for red.

Regardless of their different styles or places of production, all of the hangings would have been through many separate processes.[26] It begins with the preparation of the cloth by steeping it in oil or a fatty substance like buffalo milk, to ensure its smoothness for drawing on, and also to minimise seeping of the outlines, colours and mordants as they are applied. All the cloths were treated with a solution made from one of a number of alum-bearing plants in order to provide the natural fixative or mordant that is essential to the fast, red dyes so characteristic of South India. They were dyed with a local red dye, usually chay (*Oldenlandia*

4. A contemporary artist works with the *kalam*, made of bamboo and string

umbellata), but sometimes a locally available substitute. Some of them were also dyed with local indigo, which necessitates resisting the cloth with wax in order to shield those parts of the textile that are not required to be blue. Some pieces (cat. 2 and cat. 9) show telltale blue streaks where the wax resist has cracked and allowed small amounts of the blue dye to penetrate to the cloth. Resist-dyeing is present in almost all of the cloths, not only where indigo is used; it can enable white lettering to appear against a red background or provide an undyed outline to separate the figures from their background (see cat. 6–8). The various stages of producing a *kalamkari* in modern-day Srikalahasti are illustrated by the series of samples produced by Gurappa Chetty in 1981 (see ill. 5).

Technically the least complex of the group are the Tamil pieces (cat. 6–8, 10–11 and 15–18). The designs are large in scale, with little detail, and the palette is restricted to a range of earthy reds, ochre and black. There is no use of indigo blue. The deep reddish-brown dye is almost certainly that described by E.B. Havell in his survey (see p. 15). Havell's description of the dye process at Madurai is noticeably different from that of most accounts of the South Indian *kalamkari*: instead of the usual South Indian red dye, chay, he describes a local plant called *tinbura* root being used, together with the ashes of a coastal plant called *Salicornia indica* (a type of samphire) and, for the all-important mordant, the aluminium-rich plant *Memecylon tinctorium* (sometimes called 'saffron tree'), as well as gingelly oil (a type of sesame oil) to enable the cloth to be smooth enough to draw on and to minimise seeping of the lines and colours.

The black outlines of the figures would be drawn first on the prepared cloth, using the *kalam* fitted for this purpose with a double metal tip. In a rare survival, this initial drawing can be seen on the reverse of cat. 6 (see ill. 6 on p. 19). Evidently this drawing was abandoned and the design was started again on the other side, probably because the artist started the story at the wrong place: in the finished cloth, the episodes shown on the reverse are present, but on the third register rather than the first. The white inscriptions on these pieces would be written with the *kalam* using a wax resist so that when dyeing occurred the letters would remain white against the red ground. The white outlines separating the figures from the red-brown background in several of the cloths in this group would be achieved by leaving the outlines of the figures free of the mordanting material when it was applied with a brush around them.

The Sri Lankan *Ramayana* hanging (cat. 5) is unusual amongst the nineteen hangings as it has no resist-dyeing at all. The background is an undyed light brown, allowing the figures and the inscriptions to be simply drawn with the *kalam* on to it. The rust-red dye and its mordant would probably have been applied with a brush, as would the

5. Stages of manufacturing of a *kalamkari*. Made by Gurappa Chetty, Srikalahasti, 1981–82, V&A, IS 18-1982.

6. Balakanda from Madurai (reverse), IM 24-1911, 19th century (cat. 6)

black, ochre and even small patches of pale indigo, which could also be surface-applied rather than vat-dyed, to produce this weak shade.

An abundant use of deep, resist-dyed indigo and patches of bright yellow are characteristics of modern and historic work from Srikalahasti (cat. 3, 4 and 19), together with masterful drawing of often very complex scenes, such as cat. 19. But the most remarkable and technically complex are the large hangings from the coastal region (cat. 1, 2 and 9). These pieces, with their white backgrounds, delicate drawing and expert use of red (mostly from the chay root but also, according to Havell [1889: 16], *Morinda citrifolia*, locally called *al* or *chiranjee*) and indigo blue dyes, recall the finest of the chintz fabrics made for export to Europe and to South-East Asia. This is not surprising, as these temple hangings come from the same part of South-East India (the northern part of the Coromandel Coast) and were very likely made by the same communities or even the same craftspeople that produced those remarkable export pieces. In places, we can even see hints of this when flowering trees with clear links to those found on export pieces occur as space-fillers or to mark the end of a story (see cat. 2, fig. 51.1). Different shades of red and pink are created by expert manipulation of mordant solutions. Yellow, a notoriously difficult colour to dye well in India, is painted directly onto the surface. Amongst various possible yellow dyes, it is worth noting Havell's observation of the use of the galls of *Terminalia chebula* (myrabolan or gall-nuts) for this purpose, for what he calls Masulipatam palampores, i.e. chintzes for local use as well as export to Europe, Iran and South-East Asia. Myrabolan is more usually known as an astringent and tannin-bearing element that reinforces the mordanting process rather than providing a dye.

THE V&A COLLECTION OF TEMPLE CLOTHS

The nineteen pieces described in this book were acquired between the mid-19th century and 1983. The four earliest acquisitions (cat. 2, 5, 9 and 10) were formerly in the collection of the India Museum, the institution founded by the East India Company in 1799 to house the various products of the subcontinent. In 1879, the majority of the India Museum's 20,000 objects were transferred to the care of the then South Kensington Museum, which was re-named the Victoria and Albert Museum in 1899. The India Museum material was re-numbered when it came to South Kensington Museum, and unfortunately much of the original documentation for these pieces was lost or destroyed in the transfer process. We therefore know nothing about the provenance or date of manufacture of these four pieces other than the fact that they were in the Indian Museum prior to 1879. From the evidence of other pieces that have retained some of their original documentation, we know that many textiles in the India Museum collection were acquired from the International Exhibitions that took place in both India and Europe following the Great Exhibition in London in 1851, and it is quite possible that these temple cloths were purchased from one of these, perhaps the Paris Expositions of 1855 or 1867.

Catalogue numbers 1 and 12–14 were collected by Caspar Purdon Clarke on his buying mission to India in 1881–82. Clarke had been sent to India by the museum authorities with a budget of £5,000, specifically in order to acquire examples of contemporary manufactures and to record their places of manufacture and purchase.[27] He sent back to London 3,400 objects in all media, including some 700 textiles, which were accessioned in 1883. The acquisition register states that Purdon Clarke acquired the four temple cloths in Masulipatam, for £2 (cat. 12), £1.10 shillings (cat. 13), a meagre 2 shillings and sixpence (cat. 14) and the relatively large sum of £8.10 shillings for cat. 1. The iconography of cat. 12 and cat. 13 was clearly (and not surprisingly) unfamiliar to him, as the two Ganga cloths were described as showing Shiva in the centre, and the description for cat. 12 records that "all around are scenes from the mythological and legendary history of India". The iconography of cat. 1 was more readily identifiable and was correctly described as showing scenes from the *Ramayana*.

The other 19th-century acquisition was cat. 3, which was purchased for £6 from the Colonial and Indian Exhibition held in London in 1886. It was described at the time as showing scenes from the *Ramayana* with Vishnu and Lakshmi in the centre—actually Rama and Sita. The piece is recorded as coming from North Arcot, Madras Presidency, and its more recent attribution to Srikalahasti does not conflict with this provenance.

The distinctive group of eight Tamil hangings (cat. 6–8, 11 and 15–18) was acquired by the V&A in 1911, but they had already been on loan at South Kensington Museum from 1880 to 1896. (cat. 10, another of this type, was already in the India Museum by this time.) They were purchased in 1911 for £5 each from A. Fleming, an antique dealer in Southsea, England, who described them as representing the Coronation of Rama "and other incidents in Indian history". In his letter offering them for sale to the museum, Fleming notes, "they were originally [*sic*] the property of the Late General Sir Arthur Ellis (King Edward's Equerry) to whom they were presented by a Maharajah. Sir Arthur sold them in about 1878 to the late Vincent J. Robinson, who lent them in 1880 to the South Kensington Museum, where they were exhibited in the Indian Section until 1896." Fleming also notes that "they are in perfect condition with translations sewn on the back by V.J. Robinson," who was a prominent London dealer and collector. Sadly, these translations became detached from the hangings and are now lost, but the inscriptions have been newly translated for the present book. In his recommendation for their purchase in February 1911, Stanley Clarke (Caspar Purdon Clarke's son and head of the Indian Section of the V&A) quoted George Birdwood's remarks in *Industrial Arts of India* (p. 258): "At Madura large quantities of the stained cloths for which it is celebrated are manufactured… They are made chiefly for the service of the temples and <u>are very rare to get, except by favour of the priests</u> [Stanley Clarke's emphasis]". He adds: "Apart from their industrial and ethnographical value, as designs the cloths are certainly thoroughly representative of the Dravidian (Tamil) school."

The remaining two pieces (cat. 4 and cat. 19) were acquired much more recently. Catalogue number 4 is unusual in that it has English rather than Telugu or Tamil inscriptions. It was bought in India in 1915 by Second Lieutenant Henry Castree Hughes from "a village consisting of three temples, some good craft shops and little else".[28] Unfortunately he does not give the name or the location of the village.

The most recent *kalamkari* to enter the collection is the remarkable hanging depicting the life of Christ (cat. 19). This was made by national award-winner Gurappa Chetty at Srikalahasti in 1981, and acquired by the V&A from the exhibition 'Living Arts of India' held at London's Serpentine Gallery as part of the Festival of India in 1982. The life of Christ has now become a popular subject for *kalamkari* artists in Srikalahasti, inspired by Gurappa Chetty's imaginative interpretation.

Notes

1. For example, the well-known hanging formerly in the AEDTA collection and now in the Musee Guimet (see Gittinger 1982: 121–127; Michell 1995: 250–252; Crill 2015: 136–7).
2. See for example, Guy 1998: fig. 147; Barnes, Cohen and Crill 2002: cat. 14.
3. The South Kensington Museum was renamed The Victoria and Albert Museum in 1899.
4. Irwin and Hall 1971: 70–74, col. pl. IX.
5. *Ibid.*, p. 66.
6. See Dallapiccola 2010: 270–277.
7. Calico Museum, Ahmedabad, no. 37 (Irwin & Hall 1971: 76–77, pl. 41).
8. British Museum, Asia 1991, 0327, 01 (Dallapiccola 2010: 252–258).
9. See Thangavelu 1998 for a discussion of the epic and its performance.
10. Bernier, F. 1891: 362.
11. "There is a great Trading there in *Chites* [chintz], because, besides those that are made there, a great many are brought from *St Thomas*, which are much finer and better Colours than those of the other part of the Indies." Jean de Thevenot [1666], quoted in Sen 1949: 146.
12. The master dyer Panchakalla Pedda Subbarayudu prepared the *Ramayana* canopy (2103-1883 IS; see cat. 1) in Chirala, near Guntur (Andhra Pradesh), the *Ganga duppati* (2102-1883 IS; see cat. 12) in Bandaru (Machilipatnam), and the Mahalakshmi (2104-1883 IS; see cat. 14). The other Ganga *duppati* (1759-1883 IS; see cat. 13) was also prepared in Bandaru, by Koppala Subbarayudu of Irapalli. All four works bear the date 1881/82.
13. Hadaway 1917: 14. It had been suggested by Margaret Hall that cat. 1 (2103-1883 IS) may have been made in Pallakollu (Hall 1978: fig. 5), presumably on the basis of its superior quality, and also its stylistic similarity to the pieces attributed to Pallakollu by Hadaway (Hadaway 1917: figs. 48, 49 and 53). Subsequent reading of the inscriptions has identified its place of manufacture as Chirala, which, like Pallakollu, is in the river delta region around Machilipatnam rather than further down the Coromandel Coast. Hall's attribution was therefore close to the actual place of production.
14. Havell 1889: 14.
15. *Journal of Indian Art*, vol. III, no. 27, 1889.
16. Hadaway 1917: 17.
17. See Cohen 2006.
18. See Perera 1916.
19. *Ibid.*, fig. 92.
20. A hanging in the National Museum, New Delhi, which has been attributed to South India (illustrated in Jayakar, 1978: fig. 12) has the same spotted background and may perhaps be tentatively re-attributed to Sri Lanka. A fragment in a very similar style is illustrated in Hadaway 1917: fig. 21.
21. *Census of India 1961*: 54.
22. *Census of India 1961*: 40.
23. Havell 1889: 10, 16.
24. Havell 1889: 12.
25. Birdwood 1880: 258.
26. Several detailed accounts of the processes involved in the *kalamkari*, or chintz, technique have been published. These include Havell 1889: 12–16; Hadaway 1917: 5–10; Irwin and Brett 1970: 7–12 and Appendix A, B and C; Jayakar 1978: 129–134; Mohanty et al 1987: 100–145. These all vary slightly according to the craftsman and the region under observation.
27. Caspar Purdon Clarke also managed to collect some important early items as well, including 24 pages from the 16th-century Mughal manuscript, the *Hamzanama*.
28. V&A Registry, RP 77/64.

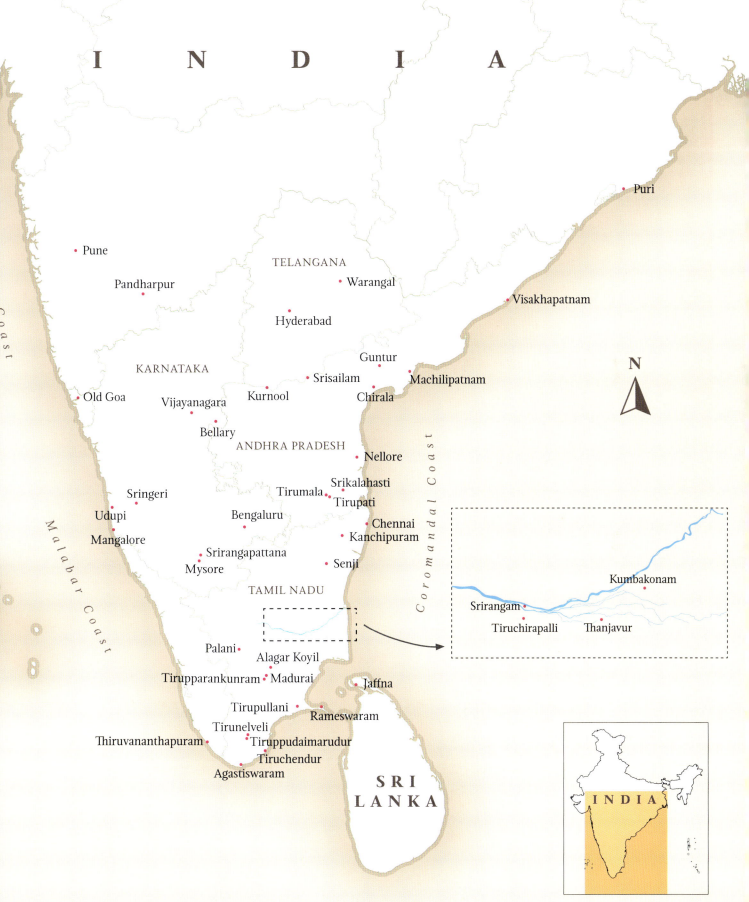

The *Ramayana*: 'Constructed, Killed and Brought'

This Telugu proverb summarizes in three words the story of Rama: he constructed (the causeway to Lanka), he killed (Ravana) and brought (Sita).[1] In every part of the subcontinent, this story, in which Rama marries Sita, chases the golden deer, beats Ravana, regains his wife, and, eventually, returns to Ayodhya to be crowned, is retold in many different ways. Thus, there is not "the" *Ramayana* but innumerable *Ramayanas*, as each time that the story is retold the narrator will inevitably stress one episode or another to make his/her point.[2]

The collection of the Victoria and Albert Museum has eight *kalamkaris*, hangings and canopies, inspired by the story of Rama. The visual treatment of the narrative can be divided in two categories: the *sampurna*, i.e. 'full', *Ramayana*, that shows the entire story from beginning to end, and the 'episodic' *Ramayana*, which deal with a specific section of the poem. Both categories are represented here. To the first belong two canopies from Coastal Andhra, two hangings from Srikalahasti, and one from Sri Lanka; to the second, three items, all from Tamil Nadu.

In no way repetitive except, perhaps, for the frame story, these *kalamkaris* offer an exciting insight in the art of storytelling. Looking at the different interpretations of the master narrative, which is attributed to a single author, the seer Valmiki,[3] one becomes aware of the infinite possibilities in which the Rama story can be retold.

In the course of the centuries the Valmikian narrative was disseminated throughout the subcontinent: countless versions of it were retold in the regional languages, individual scenes were expanded, subplots were added, and occasionally, incidents omitted. Passages which troubled the viewers, such as for instance, Vali's death, or Shurpanakha's mutilation, were explored in search of meaningful explanations.

'Anti-*Ramayanas*' were retold, completely subverting the Valmikian model: among these are the Buddhist *Dasharatha jataka*, dating of the 3rd century BCE,[4] and the *Paümacharya* by Vimala Suri, a 3rd century CE work, which adapts the story to Jaina religion and ethics. This tradition continued until the recent past, e.g. in the work of the Bengali author Michael Madhusudhan Dutt (1824–1873). His *Meghnad Bodh Kavya*, 'Saga of Meghnad's Death', published in 1861, focuses on the death of Ravana's son Meghnada (Indrajit), who is seen as a hero, a patriot, a caring son and a loving husband. In the 1950s, a 'reverse' reading of the Rama story, albeit in an extreme nationalist key, was popularized by E.V. Ramasami: its hero is Ravana rather than Rama.[5] As testified by recent events, the *Ramayana* is read and interpreted to suit the political and social contexts.

Occasionally, the role of characters especially appealing to the audiences were further elaborated into substantial digressions, almost mini-epics in their own right, which did not subvert the main narrative, but enriched it. Certain stories were popular in specific areas, e.g. the story of Rishyashringa's seduction was popular in Odia art since the 9th–10th century CE. It appears, however, for the first time in writing, in the last quarter of the 15th century in the Odia version of the *Mahabharata* by Saraladasa.[6]

Among the cluster of stories focusing on Hanuman's adventures, is the saga of Mayiliravana (known also as Mahiravana or Ahiravana) which is illustrated in the Sri Lankan temple hanging (see p. 91). This story appears in classics such as the 14th-century Telugu

Ranganatha Ramayana, the 6th-century *Kaushika Ramayana* by the Kannada poet Bhattaleshvara and in the Malayalam epic *Patalaramayanam* by Kottayam Keralavarman (1645–96). It has been elaborated in popular stories, dramas and puppet plays, and in more recent times in films.[7] The hero of the story is, predictably, Hanuman who by his intelligence and resourcefulness saves the situation. There are many regional variations of this narrative, most of them with embellishments and additions directed to an audience who revels in tales of magic and lurid gore. The probable aim of this mini-epos was the celebration of Hanuman. Furthermore, by inserting a series of adventures in Patala Lanka, 'subterranean Lanka', the war between Ravana and Rama assumed a new, more exciting, dimension. Last but not least it accommodated "some Tamil folk-traditions, obviously current in the oral lore, concerning the *rakshasas* of Lanka, the clan of Ravana, the deeds of Hanuman."[8]

The figure of Sita has been elaborated upon both in folk and classical narratives throughout India. A case in point is the *Adbhutaramayana*: two of its most notable variants are the events surrounding her birth, in this case as the daughter of Ravana's wife, Mandodari, as well as her conquest of Ravana's older brother, Sahasramukharavana, 'Ravana-of-the-thousand-heads', in her Mahakali form. In this work Sita is explicitly identified with Devi. Inspired by this incident, *Shatakantha* ('hundred-headed') *Ramayanas* were composed in Telugu and Tamil. The same episode is found in all Assamese, Odia and Bengali *Ramayanas*.[9]

Particularly interesting, and less known, are the retellings of the narrative from Sita's vantage point, e.g. the late-16th century Bengali *Chandrabati Ramayana*. Chandrabati wove together various folk stories and ballads into a narrative, which she never completed. She focuses on Sita highlighting her fate as a wronged woman: "abducted, rescued, doubted and returned to the forest by her devoted but suspicious husband" (Arni 2011: 151).[10]

To dwell on the many variations and permutations of this fascinating story, which inspired literature and arts of South and South-East Asia for centuries, is beyond the scope of this brief introduction. The Telugu version of an Indian proverb pointedly sums up the countless versions of the Rama story, thus: "After hearing the whole *Ramayana*, someone asked, 'What was Sita to Rama?'."[11]

Notes

1. Sarma 1973: 31.
2. Blackburn 1996: 22.
3. This attribution has been questioned by recent scholarship. The current view is that the text underwent various phases of development between the 4th century BCE and the 4th century CE. Opinions concerning the dating of the core of the poem vary between the 6th century BCE and the 3rd century CE.
4. The date is still being debated among scholars.
5. Richman 1991: 175–201.
6. Smith 2004: 93.
7. A film, *Mayiliravanan*, or *Maitreyi Vijayam*, was the third Tamil film ever produced. It was a silent movie released in 1918; its producer was Nataraja Mudaliyar. We know of at least three film versions of the story between 1931 and 1960: *Hanuman Pataal Parakram*, director unknown, (silent) 1931; *Hanuman Patal Vijay* directed by Homi Boman Wadia (Hindi) 1951; and *Hanuman Patal Vijayan* directed by Babubhai Mistri (Tamil) 1960.
8. Zvelebil 1987: xliii.
9. Sarma, *op.cit.*, 31.
10. The retelling of the *Ramayana* by women has been explored by Nabaneeta Dev Sen in her paper 'Lady sings the Blues: When Women retell the Ramayana' in *Manushi*/Issue 108 published online: http://www.ninapaley.com/Sitayana/Manushi_LadySingstheBlues.html [accessed on 22 June 2015].
11. Smith 1988: 136–137.

Ramayana Chirala

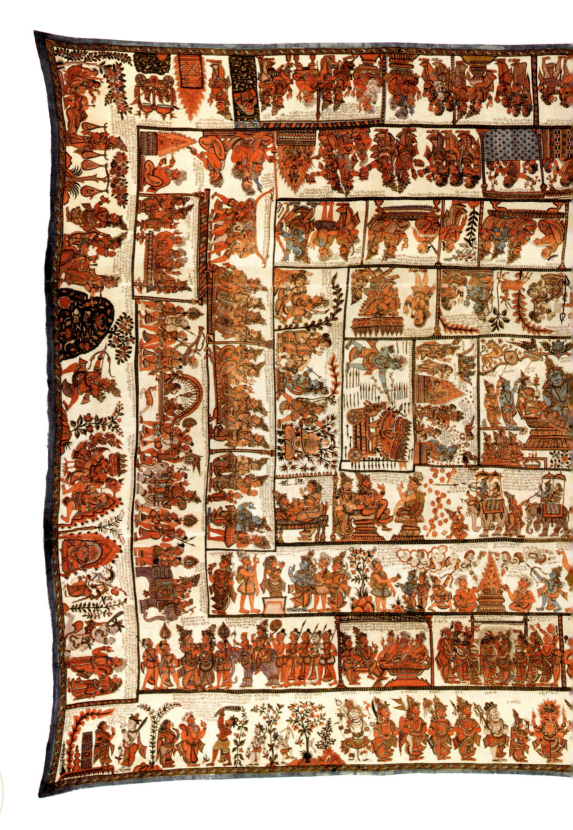

1

1. Ramayana canopy
2103-1883 (IS)
Dimensions: 296.5 x 396.5 cm
Date: c. 1881–82 (Telugu cyclical year *Vrisha*)
Artist: Panchakalla Pedda Subbarayudu
Provenance: Chirala
Captions: in Telugu

This canopy is one of the few textiles which, along with the Telugu labels, bear a date and a signature. A caption beneath the scene of the four royal weddings reads: "In the year Vrisha, in the month of Chaitra, Thursday, in Chirala, Panchakalla Pedda Subbarayudu made this *Srimad Ramayana kalamkari.*"[1]

The coastal town of Chirala (Prakasam dist., Andhra Pradesh) was, and still is, an important centre for the production of textiles. In the 13th century, Marco Polo (1254–1324) visited the port of Mutfili (Motupalli) near Paata Chirala (i.e. Old Chirala) and he mentions the flourishing weaving industry and the skills of the weaver in the production of fine varieties of textiles.[2]

The narrative in this textile, commencing on the right lower corner with an image of Vatapatrashayi (no. 1), is laid out in four concentric bands around the *Ramapattabhisheka* (coronation of Rama). This tableau is flanked by two vertical bands on either side; on the right are incidents from the *Sundarakanda* (nos. 48, 51), and on the left, scenes from the *Yuddhakanda* (nos. 52, 53).

What is striking in this and the other *Ramayana* canopy (cat. 2) is the emphasis on the events leading to the birth of Dasharatha's four sons: Rama, Lakshmana, Bharata, and Shatrughna. Among these are the story of a highway robber who, once redeemed, was to be known as Valmiki, the legendary author of the *Ramayana*, as well as the ancestor of the Boya community (no. 4.6); King Dasharatha's accidental killing of the young ascetic Gudibatta[3] (no. 5.1) which leads to his being cursed to lose his son. Finally, a long sequence of scenes illustrates the life of the ascetic Rishyashringa (nos. 7–10; see fig. 10.4). The narrative of the *Balakanda* culminates in the depiction of the four royal weddings (no. 36), followed by the dramatic encounter of Rama and Parashurama (fig. 37.1).

The politics and court intrigues narrated in the *Ayodhyakanda* are cursorily touched upon. One particular scene is noteworthy: Dasharatha reclines on the bed in his palace, while Kaikeyi towers over him indicating with three extended fingers, the three favours which he owes her (no. 39), the most important of which is to exile Rama and consecrate as king her own son, Bharata.[4] The conciseness of this scene adds to its dramatic impact.

The *Aranyakanda* is limited to few scenes; among these is the relatively unknown story of Jambumali (also known as Jambukumara), Shurpanakha's son, accidentally killed by

Lakshmana (nos. 40–41, see fig. 40). In this version of the story, Shurpanakha comes to Rama's hermitage to avenge her son's death. This encounter sets in motion a chain of events which will culminate in Sita's abduction (nos. 44–45).

Omitting the *Kishkindhakanda*, the narrative jumps to the *Sundarakanda*. Hanuman meets Sita in the Ashokavana, speaks to her, is taken captive (no. 47) and appears before Ravana (no. 48). Once freed, he sets Lanka ablaze (no. 49). The *Yuddhakanda* is reduced to three scenes, the most striking of which is Sita's fire ordeal (no. 53). The central scene is a superb tableau carefully orchestrated.

The selection of episodes suggests that the patrons were mainly concerned with the representation of the *Balakanda*, which occupies almost three quarters of the canopy. This compelled the artist to be extremely selective as far as the rest of the narrative was concerned. The emphasis on the *Balakanda* is not unusual: it gave the artist ample scope to depict courtly receptions, processions, wedding ceremonies, and music and dance scenes, which would have appealed to the patrons.

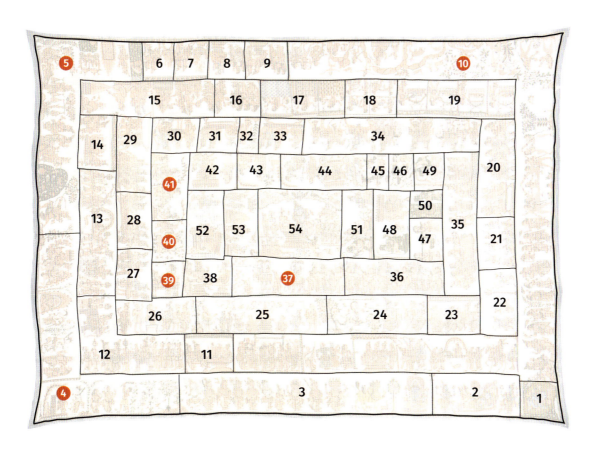

CAPTIONS

Balakanda

1. *The god* [Vishnu as Vatapatrashayi] *is lying on the vata patra in the Ocean of Milk.*

2. *Vijaya, Sridevi, Mahalakshmi, Chaturmukha Brahma, Mahavishnu reclining on the snake couch, Jaya.*

3. *When Vishnu with Mahalakshmi was resting on the Ocean of Milk, the Kalpavriksha, Kamadhenu, the Ashtadikpalas, the twenty purushas, the thirty-three crores of celestials, the ninety crores of rishis came to him, reporting that Ravana and Kumbhakarna were harassing them. The god said that in fourteen-thousand years he would be born in Dasharatha's household, and then he would kill Ravana and Kumbhakarna, putting thus an end to the difficulties which arose because of them.*
Labels: *Chaturmukha Brahma, Devendra, Agnihotra, Sahadevi, Yama, Nairriti, Varuna, Vayu, Kubera, Ishana.*

Lakshmi-Narayana holding the goddess on his left thigh, sits on the eleven-headed Shesha. Before the divine pair stand the *parijata* tree from which fall six ripe fruit, a doe (?), and Kamadhenu suckling a tiger. Behind Kamadhenu are the four-headed and eight-armed Brahma, with a diminutive fifth head emanating from his ear, and the eight *dikpalas*. The thousand-eyed Indra, the seven-armed Agni, with two heads crowned by flames, accompanied by his diminutive consort, Sahadevi, followed by Yama, and Nairriti Varuna, Vayu and Kubera are very similarly depicted: from Varuna's shoulder emerges a knotted noose, from Vayu's a fluttering flag, and from Kubera's a large sword. The last is Ishana, among whose wild hair is the Ganga.

The story of the lapsed Brahmin

4. *A Boya hunting. He hunts and fetches the birds.*

The story appears in Kamban's *Iramavataram* and probably in the Andhra *Ramayana* tradition. A lapsed Brahmin, who made his living as a hunter and highway robber, had a wife from the Boya community and a number of children.[5] Here, armed with bow and arrow he shoots at some birds perching on a flowering tree.

The Boya on his way used to attack travellers and rob them of their wealth. A deva disguised as an ascetic comes by, and when the hunter comes and wants his money [for his wife], *the ascetic says "You have committed many sins, are they your or you wife's sins? Go and ask her."*

"I committed robberies and brought you all the jewellery. You have enjoyed all this wealth. Is this sin yours or mine?" [She answers:] *"You robbed the wealth, so the sin is yours ..."* [illegible]

The Boya converses with his elegantly dressed and bejewelled wife.

Fig. 4.6   Fig. 4.5   Fig. 4.4

He returns to the rishi, prostrates himself before him and wants to know how having committed such a load of sins, he can atone for them. The rishi tells him: "Plant this stick into the ground, sit there and repeat 'Ram Ram'. When it grows branches your sins will have disappeared and you will get salvation." (fig. 4.4)

Narada arrives to the anthill and says: "Fourteen thousand years will have elapsed soon, Rama will be born in the palace of Dasharatha maharaja and then your sins will be annihilated." (fig. 4.5)

Narada arrives at the anthill inside which the Boya is practising austerities. The sage peeps through a hole and sees the Boya steeped in meditation. His body is covered by a mane of grey hair and by his unkempt beard. Near the anthill his former weapon is now bearing flowers.

Brahma arrives and writes on his tongue the bija aksharam [mystic syllable], *and gives him the name Valmiki.*[6] (fig. 4.6)

The story of Gudibatta

Just before his death, Dasharatha mentions to Kausalya that he has accidentally killed Gudibatta, and that he has been cursed by his parents to lose his own son.[7] The crucial importance of this incident has been fully recognized in both, the figurative and dramatic arts of the Telugu speaking areas, for example the *Ramayana* series carved on the inner face of the enclosure wall of the Ramachandra temple at Vijayanagara, which commences with the depiction of the killing of the young ascetic.[8]

Fig. 5 ends   Fig. 5 begins

Fig. 5.1

5. *Near a lake Dasharatha maharaja shoots an arrow at Yajnadatta [i.e. Gudibatta], mistaking him for an elephant.* (fig. 5.1)

Gudibatta fills the vessel with water from the lake.

Yajnadatta [i.e. Gudibatta] falls down and Dasharatha comes and asks: "Who are you?" He is not answering the question but replies: "My mother and father are very thirsty, please give them this pot."

King Dasharatha hunts near a lake teeming with aquatic life. A large tree on the shores of the lake prevents the king from seeing his target. His arrow hits a young ascetic who was fetching water for his parents.

Dasharatha maharaja gives the water to Gudibatta's parents.

The king walks towards a tree on which hangs the yoke with the two baskets in which sit the elderly blind parents of the killed youth and gives them the pot of water.

Dasharatha maharaja carries the yoke in which sit the parents and brings them to where Gudibatta was lying. They look at their son and become extremely sad. They curse the king saying: "One day you will experience the very same pain we are experiencing now, after having been separated from our son."

Under a tree, the dying youth rests his head on his mother's lap. His father seated behind her, lifts his arm in a gesture of despair. Both parents are in tears.

Gudibatta and his parents step into a chariot and ascend to heaven.

Dasharatha maharaja cremates Gudibatta and his parents.

Dasharatha maharaja takes a bath in the lake.

6. *Dasharatha maharaja returns to Ayodhya and talks to the seven rishis.*
   Label: *Sumantra.*

Dasharatha, on a throne, flanked by his minister, Sumantra, consults *rishi* Vasishtha.

The story of Rishyashringa

While in most pictorial renderings of the *Ramayana* this long narrative is reduced to the scene of Rishyashringa's seduction, here it is narrated in its entirety. Rishyashringa was the son of an ascetic and a doe. The animal accidentally drank some water which the sage Vibhandaka—here called Vibhanda—kept in his *ashrama*, and as a consequence became pregnant. The result of this miraculous pregnancy was Rishyashringa, 'deer-horned', a deer-headed boy. He lived in the seclusion of the forest and was educated by his father in the intricacies of Vedic lore and ritual. This peaceful life was brusquely interrupted by the arrival of a group of courtesans sent into the forest by the king of Anga, Romapada, whose kingdom was plagued by drought and who knew that only Rishyashringa's presence could bring the life-saving rain.[9] The girls seduced the youth, brought him to Romapada, and there he was married to the king's adoptive daughter, Shanta.[10]

7. *Romapada maharaja would like to know how he can end the famine. The rishis say: "If you can bring here Rishyashringa, son of Vibhanda mahamuni, the famine will cease."*

8. *They* [the *rishis*] *summon the courtesans and talk to them.*

9. *The courtesans take leave from Romapada maharaja and promise to fetch Rishyashringa.*

10. *While Rishyashringa was roaming on the mountain he sees the girls approach and runs away.*

    They arrive and conceal their jewellery and their clothes in a cave.

    They are naked, carry fruits, and run after Rishyashringa.

    In an ashrama, Vibhanda mahamuni teaches his son Rishyashringa.

    Rishyashringa plays with the deer on the Rishyashringa mountain.

    In the upper part of the tableau Rishyashringa plays with the deer. The lower part evokes the incidents leading to his birth: the doe eats what looks like a fruit, gives birth to a deer-headed boy and cleans him.

    The girl gives some fruit to Rishyashringa. (fig. 10.4)

    Rishyashringa asks the girl for the fruit.

    They [the girls] *are very nice to him and they give him the fruit. He takes it.*

    They [the girls] *seduce him.*

    Victorian propriety demanded, for this and the next scene to be hidden beneath a patch of white cloth carefully sewn onto the hanging. Only Rishyashringa's head, a female leg and hand are visible.

    They [the girls] *seduce him.*

    The girls make him sit on a palanquin and carry him [to the Anga country].

Fig. 10.4

Rishyashringa sits on a palanquin formed by the four girls who are naked except for their jewellery. While on their way to the court of Anga, he fondles the breasts of the two nearest to him.

The girls adorn him with jewellery; they let him gaze at himself in the mirror and fan him with the fan.

They put on him a flower garland. The girls make him wear ... [illegible]

The girls bring Rishyashringa along with them.

Romapada maharaja comes with his forces to meet Rishyashringa, pays his respects and takes the sage with him.

The king is first shown greeting the sage with cupped hands and then prostrating himself at his feet and touching them with his hand. Behind Romapada is a fierce-looking soldier in a short lower garment, hair tied in a topknot and armed with a long spear.[11]

Romapada maharaja is taking Rishyashringa to his country.

Romapada maharaja and his army carry him in a palanquin to their country.
Label: *Rishyashringa.*

Romapada maharaja invites the kings of all the fifty-six[12] countries to celebrate Rishyashringa's marriage.

Drums and pipes are played, and dancing girls dance.
Labels: *Tittigaru* (bagpipe player), *Maddalagaru* (drummer) *Talagaru* (player of cymbals), *Bhogastrilu* (courtesan).

10 [ends] *Brahmins throw akshate* [sanctified rice]; *Rishyashringa marries Shanta Devi; Brahmins throw akshate.*

Fig. 10 begins

Fig. 10 ends

11. *Dasharatha maharaja requests the seven rishis to perform the putrakameshti yaga [a complex sacrifice to ensure the birth of a son]. They say that Rishyashringa is in the country of Romapada maharaja and as soon as he will come, they will perform the yaga.*

    In Ayodhya, King Dasharatha, flanked by his minister Sumantra, converses with a group of ascetics.

12. *Dasharatha maharaja meets Romapada maharaja with his army.*

    He greets Romapada maharaja and hugs him.

13. *Romapada maharaja hears that Dasharatha maharaja is on the way to his country and, accompanied by his army, goes to meet him.*

    Dasharatha maharaja takes Rishyashringa with him.

    Rishyashringa and Shanta Devi are brought in a palanquin to Ayodhya.
    Labels: *Shanta Devi, Rishyashringa.*

14. *The seven maharishis sit together and discuss the details of the putrakameshti yaga.*
    Labels: *[from left] Sumantra, Dasharatha maharaja, Vasishtha, Rishyashringa.*

15. *All the rishis sit and perform the putrakameshti yaga.*

    The seven maharishis perform the putrakameshti yaga.

16. *Agnihotra* [i.e. Agni] *gives the payasa* [sweet dish] *to Rishyashringa.*

    Rishyashringa takes the payasa and hands it over to Dasharatha maharaja.

    Dasharatha brings the payasa and shares it among his three wives: Kausalya, Kaikeyi and Sumitra.

17. *Kausalya is giving birth. Kaikeyi is giving birth. Sumitra is giving birth.*

    The three queens, each assisted by two servants, are in labour. Tears flow from their eyes while they clutch with all their strength to ropes hanging from the ceilings. Screens of *ikat*, tie-dyed material, and printed cloth, cover their bodies from the waist down.

18. [Anti-clockwise from right:] *Kausalya's baby is being bathed. Kaikeyi's baby is being bathed. Sumitra's baby is being bathed. Nanny is giving a bath to the baby.*

19. [From right:] *Kausalya sings to the baby in the cradle.*

    Kaikeyi sings to the baby in the cradle. Sumitra sings to the baby in the cradle.

    Nanny sings to the baby in the cradle.

20. [From right:] *Sumitra's sons Lakshmana and Shatrughna.*

    Kaikeyi's son, Bharata; Kausalya's son, Sri Rama. Vasishtha is naming Dasharatha maharaja's sons. The seven maharishis.

    King Dasharatha and his three queens celebrate the naming ceremony of their sons.

21. [Lower register:] *Vasishtha maharishi teaches the four boys.*
    Labels: [from left] *Sri Rama, Bharata, Lakshmana, Shatrughna.*
    Labels: [upper register, from right] *Lakshmana, Rama, Shatrughna, Bharata.*

22. *Sri Rama and Lakshmana practise archery. Bharata and Shatrughna practise archery.*

23. *Vishvamitra comes and takes Rama and Lakshmana away with him.*
    Labels: *Sumantra;* [in the box] *Dasharatha maharaja.*

    The sage Vishvamitra arrives in Ayodhya and requests Dasharatha to let Rama and Lakshmana go with him in the wilderness. the king discusses with the sage. Rama and Lakshmana, armed with bows and arrows, stand between them.

24. *Vishvamitra commands* [Rama] *to kill* [the demoness] *Tataki. Sri Rama turns* [his face] *to the other side and attacks Tataki. Tataki falls down dead.*
    Label: [above the demoness] *Tataki*

    The artist depicts Rama shooting the fatal arrow without looking at Tataki, suggesting thus that his eyes will not look at any other woman but Sita.

25. *Vishvamitra tells Sri Rama that Subahu and Maricha are coming.*

    Subahu throws ... [illegible] *from the pitcher.*

Maricha takes the arrow of Rama in the middle of the seven seas and keeps it there.

Vishvamitra is performing the yaga.

Once the yaga is completed, Vishvamitra blesses Rama and Lakshmana and gives them the powerful arrows.

Labels: [from right] *Sri Rama, Agastya mahamuni, Gautama maharishi, Lakshmana Perumal, Lakshmana Perumal, Sri Rama.*

Vishvamitra asks Rama to free the *rishi*s of the forest from the harassments of Subahu and Maricha. Subahu flies overhead, carrying the head of a dead animal and a jug of spirits which he pours onto the sacrificial fire. Hit by Rama's arrow, he dies. Floating in the air, opposite Subahu, is Maricha, also carrying polluting substances. He escapes Lakshmana's arrows, and concealed in a cloud, flies away. At the centre of the scene is the sacrificial fire tended by Agastya (right) and Gautama (left) both with a pot of *ghee* in one hand and a ladle in the other. Immediately after their victory over the *rakshasas*, Vishvamitra gives the two boys the magical quiver filled with arrows.

26. *When Vishvamitra was accompanying the princes to Midanapuram, Rama's foot touched the rock. Ahalya resumed her human form.*
    Labels: *Gautama mahamuni, Lakshmana Perumal.*

    Lakshmana, Vishvamitra, and Rama walk in the forest when Rama's foot touches a pile of rocks. Ahalya, the wife of Gautama *maharishi* emerges from them and pays homage to Rama.

27. *After Ahalya was freed* [from her curse], *Sri Rama, Lakshmana and Vishvamitra resumed their journey and the emperor Janaka came to meet them to accompany them to Midanapura.*

28. *Janaka chakravarti and his brother decided that their daughters were to be given* [in marriage] *to the four sons of Dasharatha maharaja, so they decided to write a letter.*

29. *The kings of the fifty-six countries came to Midanapura.*

    [In the bow] *The rakshasas fetched the Pinaka and delivered it.*

    Four seated kings watch five *rakshasas* carrying the huge bow of Shiva, the Pinaka. The four crowned figures represent the rulers of the whole earth who have been invited to Janaka's court for the archery contest.

30. *While the kings of the fifty-six countries, all the devatas, and the whole universe were watching, Sri Rama broke the Pinaka in three pieces.*
    Labels: [from left] *Lakshmana Perumal, Vishvamitra.*

31. *After Sri Rama had broken the bow, King Janaka was overjoyed and sent an invitation to the marriage to Dasharatha maharaja requesting them to come.*

    [On the palm leaf strip:] *He* [Dasharatha] *should bring Bharata and Shatrughna.*

32. *This Brahmin carries the wedding invitation to Ayodhya.*

33. *The Brahmin reads the invitation and Dasharatha maharaja prepares to travel to Midanapura. Bharata and Shatrughna accompany him.*

34. *Dasharatha maharaja with his army, Vasishtha muni, Bharata, Shatrughna, and his [Dasharatha's] wives goes to Midanapura.*

    Janaka maharaja embraces Dasharatha maharaja. Janaka maharaja goes to meet Dasharatha maharaja.
    Labels: [to the extreme right] *Bharata, Shatrughna.*

    On the right, Dasharatha sits on an elephant driven by a diminutive mahout wielding a large *ankusha*. He is followed by a standard bearer, and by Bharata and Shatrughna on horses. At the centre of the tableau, Janaka and Dasharatha meet and embrace each other. To the extreme left is Janaka riding his elephant, followed by a standard bearer.

35. *The kings of the fifty-six countries are being entertained by the dancing girls at court.*

36. *Sita [weds] Sri Rama, Malavika [weds] Bharata, Urmila [weds] Lakshmana, Shrutakirti [weds] Shatrughna.*

37. *After the wedding Sri Rama travels to Ayodhya, and on the way meets Parashurama. The latter says: "I am Rama and you are Rama; there should be no two Ramas." Saying so, he hands his bow over to Rama.* (fig. 37.1)

    Sri Rama takes the bow and the arrow, shoots the arrow which makes a deafening sound, and the bow breaks.

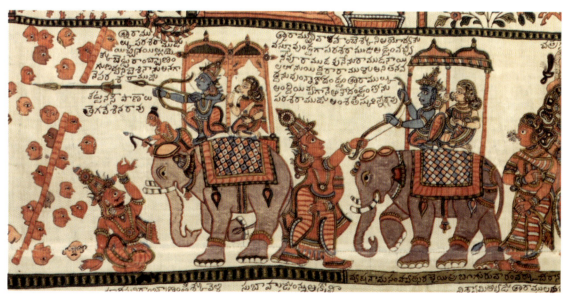

Fig. 37.1

This episode is drawn from the *Ranganatha Ramayana*: King Dasharatha, the four young couples, and their entourage, on their way to Ayodhya are confronted by Parashurama. He challenges Rama to fight him. Rama is, however, troubled at the idea, and says so. Parashurama then gives him his own bow and requests him to string it. Rama has no difficulty in lifting and stringing the bow, and aims an arrow at him. Parashurama, fearing for his life, asks Rama to demolish the staircase he built by piling up the bodies of the kings he had killed, and which enabled his own ancestors to reach *svarga* easily.[13] Rama destroys the staircase.

Parashurama is dressed in courtly attire; only his long hair betrays his ascetic status. After having strung Parashurama's bow, Rama aims an arrow at what looks like a pole (it should really be a ladder), breaking it into two. Twenty-six severed heads fly around the pole.

Cartouche beneath 36 and 37: *In the year Vrisha, in the month of Chaitra (March–April), Thursday, in Chirala, Panchakalla Pedda Subbarayudu made this Srimad Ramayana kalamkari.*

Ayodhyakanda

38. *Dasharatha maharaja, Vasishtha and Sumantra sit together and decide that Rama should be crowned.*

39. *While Dasharatha maharaja was lying down* [his youngest queen] *Kaikeyi comes and says, "You offered me three boons. First of all you have to crown Bharata and send Rama to the forest".* (fig. 39)

Aranyakanda

The killing of Jambumali (Jambukumara) and the mutilation of Shurpanakha

40. *Lakshmana attacks Jambumali.* (fig. 40)

Fig. 39

In Valmiki's and Kamban's versions of the story, Shurpanakha comes to Rama's hermitage as if by chance. According to the Telugu versions of *Ramayana*, she comes to avenge the death of her son, the ascetic Jambumali, accidentally killed by Lakshmana. She appears before Rama filled with anger, but, on seeing him, she falls in love.

Lakshmana, with a basket hanging from his left arm, walks towards a cluster of trees. Bow and quiver hang from his shoulder and he carries two swords.[14] While cutting his way through the thicket Lakshmana inadvertently kills Jambumali who is engaged in meditation. With his squinting eyes he looks at the sky and worships Surya. A foliage scroll separates this from the next episode.

Fig. 41.2 ← Fig. 41.1 Fig. 40

41. *Shurpanakha comes to Sri Rama. He requests her to bend down and writes on her back a message to Lakshmana: "Cut her ears and nose and let her go!"*

Lakshmana Perumal is holding her under his feet, cuts her nose and ears and lets her go. (fig. 41.2)

Shurpanakha appears before Rama, in whose hand is a large stylus with which he writes on what looks like her stomach, although the angle of head, arms, knees, feet, clothing and her whole pose seem to imply that he is writing on her back. This is corroborated by the caption which indicates that he writes on her back.[15] A stylized tree divided this from the episode's conclusion.

42. *She goes and complains to Ravana after her nose and ears were cut off.*

43. *While they [Rama and Sita] were sitting in the hut the magic deer appears in front of them and Sita asks Rama to catch it.*

44. *Ravana in disguise appears in front of her [Sita] and begs for food. She brings him fruit.*

Having inadvertently stepped outside the seven protective lines drawn onto the ground, Sita falls into Ravana's power. The seven lines are prominently shown between Ravana and Sita.

She is anguished and she is carried away.

While Ravana is abducting her in his chariot, the bird Jatayu fights against Ravana and falls down [wounded].

45. *[Rama] holds Jatayu in his hand.*

Rama stands with the extended right hand on which the remains of Jatayu are engulfed in the flames.[16]

Sundarakanda

46. *While Sita [captive] in the Ashokavana sits under a tree, Hanuman sees her, and reveals his identity.*
    Label: [near Sita] *Sitadevi*.

47. *The rakshasas took Hanuman captive, bound him and took him to Lanka.*

48. *They take Hanuman before Ravana, make him sit and he argues with Ravana. [Above the small figure:] This rakshasa threatens Hanuman.*

    Hanuman, seated on his coiled tail faces Ravana enthroned.

49. *Hanuman comes and catches the rakshasas, who were holding Sita captive, by the hair and throws them into the fire.*

    This scene is the conflation of two distinct episodes: the devastation of Ravana's gardens and the burning of Lanka. A square enclosure with four flattish domes suggests the city of Lanka. Hanuman, depicted here as a huge monkey, fights against a *rakshasa*. Hanuman's blazing tail sets fire to the walls and the buildings of Lanka before enveloping his adversary.

50. *Hanuman extinguishes the fire of his tail and cools it in the ocean.*

Yuddhakanda

51. [Near Hanuman:] *Hanuman collected Lakshmana and carried him here.*

    During the war Lakshmana falls. Rama is very worried. [The physician] Sushena comes, checks his pulse, and says there is nothing to be worried about.

52. *Sri Rama is sending his unique [i.e. magical] arrow and fights fiercely.*

    Rama, on foot, under a shower of arrows, shoots his magical arrow and kills Ravana on his chariot.

53. *Sri Rama makes Sita undergo the fire ordeal. The devatas sprinkle flowers, the kinnaras are playing music. Rambha and Urvashi are dancing. Agnihotra brings Sita, and places her next to Rama.*

    Labels: *Vibhishana* [extreme left], *Sita* [near the blazing pyre].

Ramapattabhisheka

54. **Labels:** [from left] *Shatrughna, Bharata, Sita Ammavaru, Pattabhisheka Rama, Vasishtha, Vishvamitra, Bharadvaja, Gautama, Jamadagni, Kashyapa, Atreya mahamuni and Lakshmana.*

Notes

1. The master dyer Panchakalla Pedda Subbarayudu was extremely versatile: the Ganga 'duppati' in cat. 12 (pp. 135–145) testifies to his ability to work in the most different styles.

2. Polo 1928: 185–87

3. There seems here to be a slip of the pen: in no. 5 the youth is called Yajnadatta, which is the name of his father, but elsewhere in this work he is called Gudibatta; generally he is known as Shravanakumara.

4. According to the tradition current in Andhra, the boons Dasharatha had promised Kaikeyi when she helped him on the battlefield are three, instead of the usual two.

5. The Boya are an old fighting community, who played a major role in the Carnatic Wars. They were renowned fighters, hunters and sportsmen.

6. Because he emerged from a *valmika*, white anthill, he is Valmiki.

7. *The Ramayana of Valmiki*, Vol. II: *Ayodhyakanda* (Pollock, S.I., trsl.), sarga 57–58, 1986: 204–210. See also Sarma 1973: 130.

8. Dallapiccola, 'Ramayana in Southern Indian Art' 2011: 183–184. The same applies to shadow puppet theatre. I had an opportunity of witnessing two performances of the *Sita kalyana* (1994 and 2001) by puppeteers from the Bellary district in Karnataka. In both cases the story of Gudibatta, also known as Shravanakumara, was the first episode in the play.

9. The connection between Rishyashringa and the rain endures. In 2009, on a visit to Kigga, a small village near Sringeri (Chikmagalur dist., Karnataka) I was told that this is the place where Rishyashringa is deemed to have merged into the Shiva *linga* enshrined in the Sri Rishyashringeshvara Temple. Even today, the Jagadguru of Sringeri Sharada Pitham performs a *puja* at Kigga to ensure rainfall, or to avoid floods.

10. Shanta was the daughter of King Dasharatha and Kausalya. The childless Romapada, king of Anga, came to Ayodhya on a visit, and being a great friend of Dasharatha he entreated him to give Shanta to him as a foster daughter.

11. The hairstyle, occasionally the hair is shaved but for the topknot, and the attire seem to suggest that this person belongs the Boya community, who were also employed as soldiers and palanquin bearers.

12. According to the South Indian tradition, there are seven countries in each of the eight directions of the space. Thus the expression 'fifty-six countries' denotes the totality of the earth.

13. Srinivas 2005: 51, ill. 86.

14. Surya sent a sword to Jambumali as a reward for his austerities. The weapon remained unclaimed as Jambumali expected Surya to hand it over to him personally. Lakshmana seeing a sword hanging in the air took it. For a full account of the story of Jambumali, see Sarma 1973: 87–88.

15. The detail of Rama writing the letter to Lakshmana on Shurpanakha's back is explicitly mentioned in the Malay version of the *Ramayana*, the *Hikayat Seri Rama* written between the 13th and the 17th century and in Giridhara's 18th-century version in Gujarati. Personal communication by Mrs. M. Brockington, 15 February 2015.

16. The *Hikayat Seri Rama* explains this as follows: "…the bird was cremated on a funeral pyre which Seri Rama held in his arms, because no place could be found which had not been walked on by men and on which this excellent bird could have been cremated". Stutterheim [1925] 1989: 38.

Ramayana MACHILIPATNAM

This canopy was probably prepared in the area of Machilipatnam in the mid-19th century. The *Balakanda* is again depicted in detail. While the artist responsible for the Chirala *Ramayana* (cat. 1) has drastically shortened the *Ayodhyakanda* and *Aranyakanda* sections and omitted the *Kishkindhakanda,* the selection here is more inclusive, especially in the case of the *Aranyakanda*; the *Kishkindhakanda*, however, is reduced to a single illustration: the meeting between Rama and Sugriva. The narrative is laid out in four concentric rows and two horizontal bands, one below (no. 53) and one above (no. 54) the central tableau, displaying Rama's coronation, *Ramapattabhisheka*. The beginning and the end of each episode are marked by a vertical band with a decorative motif. The various phases of the action within single narrative sequence are separated by an elegant vertical wave-like motif.

The opening scene of the narrative, in which the deities and *dikpalas* pay homage to Vishnu, bears strong resemblance to the ones in cat. 1 and cat. 9 (*Krishnacharita*). It is followed by a rendering of the story of Valmiki, in which two different traditions merge (figs. 1–2).

The prologue is followed by the stories of Rishyashringa (nos. 6–13), and Gurubatta (no. 16). The order of the narrative here is slightly different from that of cat. 1: there, the incident of Gurubatta—called Gudibatta—is shown immediately after the story of Valmiki and before that of Rishyashringa. The rest of the *Balakanda* narrative follows the usual template. The *Ayodhyakanda* section has some striking rendering of landscapes, elements of which remind one of the late 18th-century palampores made for the Western market: e.g. the depiction of Guha ferrying the exiles across the Ganga, and the meeting of Rama and his brothers on Mount Chitrakuta (figs. 41–42).

The detailed *Aranyakanda* narrative begins with the failed abduction of Sita by Viradha (no. 43) followed by Lakshmana's accidental killing of Shurpanakha's son, Subahu—called Jambumali in the Chirala canopy, by Shurpanakha's mutilation (no. 45) and, finally, by the battle of Rama against Ravana's three brothers (no. 47). After Sita's abduction and Jatayu's death, Rama and Lakshmana return to the hermitage to find it deserted (fig. 49.2).

On their search for Sita the two brothers meet Kabandha, a *gandharva*, who was cursed by a sage to retain his ungainly form until they would release him from the curse (fig. 50). After having killed Kabandha, thus releasing him from his curse, the exiles meet Sabari, an ardent devotee of Rama, who advises them to go to Kishkindha. This eventful part of the narrative is limited to one pivotal scene: the

meeting of Rama and Lakshmana with Sugriva, and their pact of alliance (fig. 50.2). A small but noteworthy detail: here the artist shows Sugriva and his followers returning to Rama the jewels that Sita dropped while being abducted in Ravana's chariot.

The *Sundarakanda* and *Yuddhakanda* are arranged around the central medallion. Pride of place have the meeting of Sita and Hanuman in the Ashokavana (fig. 51), the burning of Lanka (no. 52), Indrajit's gory sacrifice in Nikumbhila, just before his battle against Lakshmana, and Vibhishana instructing Rama to aim his fatal arrow at Ravana's navel, containing the nectar of immortality (no. 53). Sita's fire ordeal (no. 55) and the return to Ayodhya in the aerial chariot, the *Pushpaka Vimana* (no. 56), conclude the narrative. The central medallion surrounded by lotus petals is slightly different in layout from the usual *Ramapattabhisheka* scenes (fig. 57).

The style of the painting is totally different from that of the Chirala canopy: it is more inventive, though not as carefully executed, but full of life and movement. The master dyer's deep empathy with the subject is revealed by the countless small details that enliven his work. Each scene bears an explanatory caption and the occasional label in Telugu.

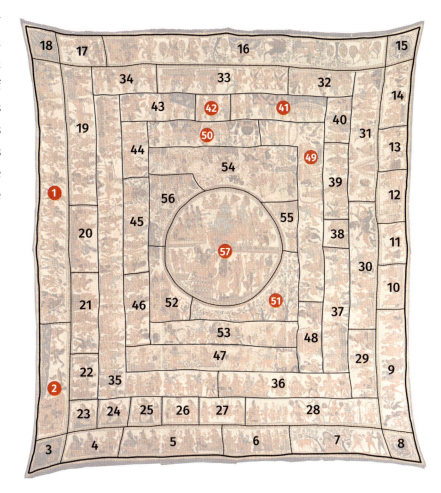

2. Ramayana canopy
5457A (IS)
Dimensions: 346 x 338 cm
Date: Probably mid-19th century
Provenance: Probably Machilipatnam
Captions: in Telugu

CAPTIONS

Balakanda

1. *Brahma and other devatas come to Srimadnarayana* [Vishnu] *to complain about Ravana's harassments. Bhudevi massages his feet. Lakshmidevi assures Brahma that soon Ravana's arrogant behaviour will come to an end.*
   Labels: *Devendra, Agni, Yamadharmaraja, Nairriti, Varuna, Vayu, Yaksharaja* [*Kubera*], *Ishanaraja, Naradamahamuni, Valmiki in the anthill, Narada peeps into the anthill.* (fig. 1)

   The goddess Lakshmi, depicted here as the intermediary between Vishnu and his devotee, Brahma, is an interesting detail which may possibly indicate a Sri Vaishnava affiliation of either the patron or the artist. Brahma is followed by the *dikpalas*, as noted in cat. 1 and cat. 9. Among them, Kubera is depicted dark skinned and with sharp fangs, probably a reference to his being the head of the *rakshasas* as well as Ravana's half-brother. Along with the *dikpalas* who pay homage to Vishnu is the divine minstrel, Narada *rishi* carrying a *vina*. Two stories relating the origin of the *Ramayana* merge here: in the first, already discussed in cat. 1, Narada discovers Valmiki—a reformed robber—buried in the anthill.[1]

   Fig. 1 ⟶

2. *Bharadvaja. Valmiki curses the hunter. He has killed the chankutta bird and his chick* [caption beneath the birds]. *The hunter is killed by Valmiki* [caption above the hunter]. (fig.2)

   The second story is narrated in Valmiki's *Ramayana*. The sage sees two *krauncha* birds sporting joyfully. Suddenly, hit by a hunter, the male bird falls to the ground. The female then starts a heartrending lament. At the sight of such cruel action, Valmiki curses the hunter.[2] On the extreme right, the hunter dies engulfed in blazing flames created by Valmiki's curse.[3]

   Fig. 2 ⟶

3. A lake with three lotuses in full bloom. All around the flowers and leaves are fish and shells.

4. *Chaturmukha Brahma requests Valmiki to write the Ramayana.*
   Label: *Bharadvaja.*

   According to this version of the narrative, Valmiki has not composed the poem in a burst of poetic inspiration caused by Brahma's writing the *bija aksharam* on his tongue (see cat. 1.4), but he obeys to a divine command.

The drought in the kingdom of Anga

5. *Romapada consults the sapta maharishi. Romapada requests the priest to calculate the auspicious muhurta* [time].
   Labels: *Sapta maharishi, Minister.*

The story of Rishyashringa

6. *Romapada and his chief minister. Romapada calls the courtesans, and requests them to bring Rishyashringa. He says that he will give away half of his kingdom* [to him].

7. *The deer drinks water from the pail. Vibandhaka mahamuni's ashram.*
   Labels: [lower label] *Naked women.* [upper label] *The women give him eatables.*

   To Vibandhaka's right a doe drinks from a pail of water, an obvious allusion to the miraculous birth of Rishyashringa. The sage had once seen the beautiful *apsara* Urvashi, had an involuntary emission of semen. It fell into the water; a doe drank the water, swallowed the semen, and in due course gave birth to Rishyashringa, a human child with the horns of a deer.

8. A *hamsa* with a flower in its beak, inscribed in a circle. The four spandrels are adorned by floral motifs.

9. *The girls conceal their saris* [in the cave] *while carrying Rishyashringa. Padmakshi and Minakshi escort Rishyashringa. Romapada greets Rishyashringa and requests him to stay with him. Romapada pays homage to him* [Rishyashringa] *by prostrating himself at his feet.*

10. *Romapada wants to find the auspicious muhurta to celebrate the wedding of his daughter with Rishyashringa.*

11. **Labels:** *Horn player, Maddalam* [drum] *player, Romapada.*

12. **Labels:** *Wedding of Rishyashringa, Brahmin.*

13. **Labels:** *Horn player, Maddalam players, Shenai* [wind instrument] *player.*

14. *The dancing girls dance for Rishyashringa's wedding.*
    Labels: *Minister, Tala player, Maddalam player.*

15. *A hamsa with a flower in its beak, inscribed in a circle. The four spandrels are adorned by floral motifs.*

The story of Gurubatta

16. *Gurubatta carries his parents in his kavadi [yoke]; he was very thirsty, so he hangs the kavadi on the branch of a tree and leaves.*
    Labels: [the parents are] *Yajnadatta, Dharmashila; The kavadi hangs on a tree.*

    Dasharatha maharaja hunts elephants and hits them. Gurubatta fetches water from the lake. Dasharatha, thinking it was an elephant, shoots an arrow.

    The arrow penetrates Gurubatta's shoulder and he dies, still carrying the *lota* in his hand.

    Dasharatha comes and says to Yajnadatta that Gurubatta has been killed. Dasharatha carries the parents of Gurubatta. Yajnadatta. Dasharatha sets fire to the three of them.
    Labels: [parents in the *kavadi*] *Dharmashila and Yajnadatta.*

17. *King Dasharatha and Vasishtha plan to visit Romapada's kingdom.*

18. *A lake with three lotuses in full bloom. All around the flowers and the leaves are fish and shells.*

19. *Dasharatha and Vasishtha travel to Romapada's kingdom. These are the horses pulling the chariot. They arrive in Romapada's country. Dasharatha. Romapada embraces Dasharatha. Dasharatha pays homage to Rishyashringa by prostrating himself before him.*

20. *Vasishtha and Dasharatha request Rishyashringa to perform the putrakameshti yaga.*
    Labels: *Romapada maharaja; Dasharatha.*

21. *Vasishtha performs the putrakameshti yaga. Rishyashringa receives the payasa. Rishyashringa hands the payasa over to Dasharatha.*

22. *Dasharatha gives the payasa to Kausalya, Kaikeyi and Sumitra.*

23. *Kausalya is giving birth.*

    Kausalya, flanked by two women is giving birth to Rama; her features express the effort of giving birth, and tears run from her eyes. While she steadies herself with the ropes hanging from the ceiling and pushes her son into the world, one of her attendants gives her something to drink, while the other massages her waist. To suggest the imminent birth, a baby is drawn lying in her belly.

24. *Kaikeyi is giving birth, Manthara is helping her.*
    Label: *Midwife.*

25. *Sumitradevi is giving birth.*
    Labels: [at her side] *Balika and midwife.*

26. *Kaikadevi gives a bath to Rama, Lakshmana, Bharata and Shatrughna. Kausalya pours hot water.*

27. *Kausalya swings the cradle. Rama and Lakshmana. Sumitra swings the cradle.*

28. *Sri Rama, Lakshmana, Bharata and Shatrughna are being taught by Vasishtha. This is Lakshmana; this is Bharata; this is Shatrughna. Vasishtha muni teaching. They* [Shatrughna and Bharata] *are practising. Rama and Lakshmana practise archery.*

29. *King Dasharatha sends Rama and Lakshmana away with Vishvamitra. This is Vishvamitra.*
    Labels: *Bharata and Shatrughna; Lakshmana, Sri Rama.*

30. *Lakshmanasvami. Sri Rama. Vishvamitra gives him* [i.e. Sri Rama] *the weapons. Sri Rama kills* [the demoness] *Tataka. Tataka is dead.*

    Rama, without looking at her (see also cat.1.24), shoots an arrow, killing her.

31. *Lakshmanasvami kills Subahu. Vishvamitra completes his yaga. Sri Rama protects his* [Vishvamitra's] *yaga. Sri Rama removes Ahalya's curse.*
    Labels: *Subahu's head, Maricha* [flying in the sky], *Lakshmanasvami, Vishvamitra.*

    Vishvamitra, at the side of the *agnikunda* protected by a canopy of arrows, throws offerings in the flame. Subahu and Maricha fly overhead polluting the sacrifice while Lakshmana and Rama aim their arrows at them. Subahu is killed; his large head falls by the fire pit. In the next scene, Rama, accompanied by Vishvamitra and Lakshmana, places his foot onto a rock; from it emerges Ahalya, who, freed from her curse, pays homage to Rama.

32. **Labels:** *Lakshmanasvami, Sri Rama, Janaka chakravarti, Vishvamitra, Satananda.*

    Lakshmana and Rama are seated a short distance away from Vishvamitra, Janaka, and his minister, Satananda, who are having a conversation.

33. *Janaka chakravarti asks them to bring the bow which he had. Sri Rama breaks in the middle Janaka's bow. Janaka and Vishvamitra send the invitation to Ayodhya.*
    Labels: *Sri Rama, Lakshmanasvami; Broken bow* [at the lower end of the panel].

34. *Vasishtha tells Sumantra to get ready to go to Sri Rama's wedding. The Brahmin who brings the letter, reads it aloud to Dasharatha.*

    On the *olai* [palm leaf]: *Sri Rama's wedding invitation.*

35. *Sumitradevi, Kaikadevi, Kausalya, Dasharatha travel to Rama's wedding, Vasishtha muni, Sumantra. These are the horses pulling the chariot to Mithilapuram. These are the musicians playing the five instruments for Rama's wedding. Flag carrier, Dasharatha, a sumangali* [a woman whose husband is alive]. *Sri Rama's wedding. Brahmin. Lakshamana's wedding. Brahmin, Sumangali. Bharata and Malavika's wedding. Sumangali. Janaka chakravartin. Shatrughna's wedding. Sumangali. The musicians play horn, drums and trumpet.*

36. *Seated Sumantra. Janaka sits at the side of Dasharatha maharaja. Vishvamitra. The dancing girls perform for the wedding. A dancing girl dances, a musician beats the cymbals.*
    Labels: *Drum player, bagpipe-player.*

    The girls wear the flower garland slung over the shoulder as was customary during the Maratha period (late 17th to mid-19th century).

37. *Sumantra drives the chariot. Sri Rama encounters Parashurama, and aims at his skull.*
    Labels: *Shatrughna, Bharata, Lakshmana.*

    Shatrughna, Bharata and Lakshmana sit on a chariot drawn by two horses driven by Sumantra. Parashurama appears before them and challenges Rama. He gives his bow to Rama who strings it and shoots an arrow demolishing the staircase of heads behind the sage (see cat. 1.37).

Ayodhyakanda

38. *Dasharatha looks for the auspicious time to consecrate Rama.*

39. *Sumantra comes and announces that the time has been decided. Kaikeyi asks for the boon, and for this Sri Rama has to be sent into exile to the forest. Sri Rama, Lakshmana and Sita come and take leave of Dasharatha to go to the forest.*
    Labels: *Sita Devi, Lakshmanasvami.*

40. *Lakshmanasvami, Sitadevi and Sri Rama come to take leave of Kausalya.*

41. *Lakshmanasvami, Sitadevi, Sri Rama and Guha cross the river. Lakshmanasvami and Sitadevi are in Chitrakuta, where Sri Rama gives his sandals to Bharata. Shatrughna.* (fig. 41)

    Rama, Sita and Lakshmana are ferried across the Ganga by Guha, the ferryman, who manoeuvres a long oar. While the royal trio are on Mount Chitrakuta, Bharata and Shatrughna come to visit them with the news of Dasharatha's death, and request Rama to return to Ayodhya. He, however, true to the word he gave to his father, is determined to complete the years of exile. Rama, Sita and Lakshmana, all three in tears sit on the summit of the mountain; Rama has just removed his sandals, and entrusts them to Bharata. The latter, and Shatrughna, both tearful, take leave of the exiles.

42. *Bharata keeps Sri Rama's sandals in Nandigrama. This is the throne on which they are placed. Chitrasena* [Shatrughna] *wields the chamara.* (fig. 42)

Rama's footwear, a symbol of his presence, is placed beneath an ornate metal frame on an elaborate *pitha* [pedestal]. Bharata and Shatrughna pay homage to it.

Fig. 41 ⟶ Fig. 42

Aranyakanda

43. *Rama, Sita and Lakshmana wear the jatamudi* [jatamakuta]. *Sri Rama kills Viradha.*
    Labels: *Lakshmanasvami, Sitadevi.*

    On the left, Rama and Sita bathe in the river and wash their hair which they will tie in a *jatamakuta*, a symbol of their exile status. Lakshmana stands nearby, guarding them. On the extreme right, Viradha, a huge winged creature, abducts Sita and is decapitated by Rama's arrow.

44. *Lakshmanasvami, Sitadevi and Sri Rama come to Bharadvaja muni. He* [Rama] *promises that he will protect his yaga from the rakshasas.*
    Label: *Sutikshna.*

45. *Lakshmanasvami kills Subahu* [Jambumali]. *Sitadevi. Sri Rama is approached by Shurpanakha. Lakshmanasvami cuts Shurpanakha's nose.*

    The actual killing of Subahu is not shown, the emphasis is on Shurpanakha's mutilation.

46. *Trishura, Doshana, and Khara. Shurpanakha tells them* [that Lakshmana has cut her nose].

47. *Khara, Doshana, Trishura, all three of them, fight. Sri Rama kills Khara and Doshana. Lakshmana hides Sitadevi.*

48. *Shurpanakha comes and tells her brother of her nose being cut. Ravana seeks Maricha's help.*

49. *Maricha takes the form of a deer and comes near Sitadevi. She asks Sri Rama to catch the deer and bring it to her. Sri Rama kills Maricha. Ravana takes the form of a bhikshu and approaches Sitadevi.*
    Labels: *Deer. Maricha* [in his real form]. *Sitadevi* [in the chariot].

Ravana attacks Jatayu. The empty hut. Lakshmanasvami. Sri Rama blesses Jatayu. (fig. 49)

A battle between Ravana and Jatayu ensues. The gallant bird tries to intercept the chariot's progress; severed limbs and heads are scattered all around. Jatayu is wounded.

The return of Rama to find the empty hut is not shown. The magical lines, drawn on the ground by Lakshmana to protect Sita, are, however, emphasized.[4] Instead of seven, nine lines are depicted here on an empty background set off by two decorative wavy lines. The last scene of this sequence depicts Rama discovering in a wild and rocky landscape the dying Jatayu. He blesses him, and carries in his extended left hand the blazing flame in which Jatayu's remains are cremated.[5]

Fig. 49 begins ⟶

⟶

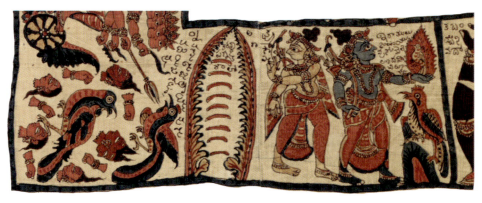

⟶ Fig. 49 ends

End of Aranyakanda; Kishkindhakanda

50. *Sri Rama and Lakshmanasvami fight with Kabandha. He [Rama] eats the fruits brought by Sabari.*

[Kishkindhakanda] He comes with Nila and Nala. Sugriva in Rishyamukha gives Sita's jewels to Rama. Rama blesses him and promises to protect him. Hanuman comes to Lakshmanasvami. (fig. 50.2)

Kabandha, who has a large head with bushy hair, dark, round eyes, wavy eyebrows, a gaping mouth filled with sharp teeth, and a lolling tongue, succumbs to the joint attack of Rama and Lakshmana, who, after having severed his arms lift them proudly in the air. In the next scene, the two princes resting under a tree are approached by the ascetic Sabari who carries a basket filled with fruit on her left shoulder. Although Sabari should be an elderly ascetic, she is shown here as a young woman.

Fig. 50.1 → Fig. 50.2

The narrative proceeds with the meeting of Rama and Lakshmana with Nila and Sugriva in the hilly region of Kishkindha. A sacrificial fire symbolizing the pact of alliance between Rama and Sugriva burns between the two parties. Sugriva hands over to Rama Sita's jewels. In the last scene of this sequence Lakshmana talks to Hanuman.

From this point on, the narrative is arranged around the central tableau. The sequence of the episodes is not in chronological order.

Sundarakanda

51. *Hanuman sits on the ashoka tree. Rakshasa keeping guard. Hanuman comes to greet Sita.* (fig. 51.1)

Rakshasa and Hanuman in the Ashokavana. All the rakshasa guards are killed by Hanuman.

Fig. 51.1

52. *Hanuman climbs on all the towers and destroys the whole of Lanka. Hanuman. The ocean, where he is cooling his tail.*

53. *Indrajit performs a homa in Nikumbhila. Lakshmanasvami kills Indrajit. Lakshmanasvami. Bear. Vibhishana tells him [i.e. Rama] the secret. Rama kills Kumbhakarna. Sugriva kneels before Rama.*

Indrajit sits opposite the sacrificial fire in which are visible a severed human head, the head of a horse and a number of dismembered body parts. In the next scene, Lakshmana sits on Hanuman's shoulder and aims an arrow at Indrajit who is riding his magical chariot. In the background arrows criss-cross the sky. The last scene of this register shows Vibhishana, recognizable by his huge club, saying something to Rama, and the king of the bears, Jambavan. Sugriva kneels before Rama while the hero shoots a volley of arrows at Kumbhakarna, a black figure with a large head. Rama's arrows have already severed his arms, one of his legs and one of his feet, and eventually the last shot decapitates him. His large head with half-closed eyes and a large mouth filled with sharp teeth lies on the ground to the extreme left. The background is filled with arrows flying in every direction.

54. *Angada kills Kumbudu [bottom left]. Angada kills Mahakaya. Lakshmanasvami kills Adikaya. Nila. Bhuta collecting Ravana's heads. Sri Rama kills Ravana.*

On a background of flying arrows, severed heads and limbs, a number of fights are in progress. In the left corner Angada, armed with a mountain peak, kills Kumbudu, who collapses to the ground still clasping his buckler. Then he kills Mahakaya by hurling a stone at him and kicking him in the stomach. Lakshmanasvami, assisted by two *vanaras*, i.e. monkeys, kills Adikaya, who, from a chariot, shoots volleys of arrows at him. To the right, Rama proceeds at full speed against Ravana, standing on a horse-drawn chariot and preceded by a foot soldier. Rama kills him with a flame tipped arrow. At the centre of the composition, dark complexioned *bhuta* (goblin) flies above the carnage of the battlefield and collects Ravana's severed heads, still bearing the crowns.

55. Sita stands in *anjali mudra* on the blazing pyre, while Rama and Lakshmana, seated on a low *asana*, watch her impassively. From the sky a winged *apsara* flies towards the pyre, showering on it a basketful of flowers.

56. *They are in the Pushpaka Vimana: Lakshmanasvami, Vibhishana, Sugriva, Hanuman. Upstairs: Sri Rama and Sitadevi.*

The *Pushpaka Vimana*, an aerial conveyance, is shown as a two-storeyed building on lotus-like wheels and provided with wings. Seated in it are the main characters of the narrative. Flanking the chariot, to the right, a *gandharva* empties a basketful of petals on the route of the *Pushpaka Vimana*.

Ramapattabhisheka

57. *Brahma chants mantras; Sarasvatidevi; the sapta maharishis sprinkle pushpavarsha [rain of flowers]. Anjaneya is holding [Rama]svami's foot. Nila and Jambavan [behind Anjaneya], Vibhishana and Sugriva chant mantras. Angada, Sumantra, Sushena, Shatrughna, Lakshmana, Bharata. (fig. 57)*

Fig. 57

Notes

1. See the story of the reformed highway robber cat. 1, p.30.
2. Valmiki discovers that his compassion has taken the melodious rhythm of a beautiful shloka. *The Ramayana of Valmiki* Vol I: 1984: 127–128.
3. The popular notion is that incurring the wrath of an ascetic spells doom.
4. This is a detail drawn from the *Ranganatha Ramayana*. Before leaving the hermitage in search of Rama, Lakshmana draws seven lines around it and warns Sita not to go beyond them. These seven lines will protect her from every peril. Srinivas 2005: 107.
5. See cat. 1, n. 16.

Ramayana SRIKALAHASTI

Ramayana Srikalahasti

This hanging was purchased from the Colonial Indian Exhibition in 1886 and is a classic example of the stylistic and iconographic conventions followed in the second half of the 19th century by the master dyers of the Srikalahasti area.[1]

The narrative, which begins with a Ganesha *puja* scene, is laid out on eleven registers arranged around the central tableau displaying Rama's coronation, the *Ramapattabhisheka*. While the artists responsible for the canopies from Coastal Andhra dwell on details of the story, especially in the *Balakanda*, the masters of the Srikalahasti area tend to propel the narrative ahead. Each scene bears a detailed description which, in general, is more informative than its actual visual rendering.

The narrative follows the usual template with some interesting variations: for instance, the accidental killing of the young ascetic by Dasharatha, the killing of Subahu, and the meeting of Rama and Parashurama have been omitted.

All the Srikalahasti works examined follow the *Ranganatha Ramayana*, according to which King Dasharatha celebrates the most prestigious of royal rituals, *ashvamedha yaga*, the horse sacrifice (fig. 9), besides the *putrakameshti yaga*, the sacrifice to ensure the birth of a son. Although the *Ayodhyakanda* is limited to few scenes, Manthara's conversation with Kaikeyi (fig. 26) resulting in Rama's banishment is vividly rendered.

The *Aranyakanda* commences with Shurpanakha's episode, omitting Lakshmana's accidental killing of Jambumali, and culminates in the abduction of Sita and the death of Jatayu.

3. Ramayana from Srikalahasti
75-1886 (IS)
Dimensions: 399.75 x 380.5 cm
Date: late 19th century
Provenance: Srikalahasti
Captions: in Telugu

The *Kishkindhakanda* is remarkably well represented by the duel between Vali and Sugriva, the killing of Vali, Vali's cremation, Sugriva's coronation, and ends with Rama entrusting his signet ring to Hanuman leaving on his expedition to Lanka. All these incidents are not shown in cat. 1 and cat. 2. Included here is also Hanuman's encounter with Lankini, the patron deity of Lanka, a rarely illustrated incident (fig. 49).

The *Yuddhakanda* is treated in much greater detail than in cat. 1 and cat. 2. This section of the narrative opens with the building of the bridge, immediately followed by a last ditch attempt to avoid a war through Angada's diplomatic mission to Ravana (fig. 58).[2] It fails, and the battle commences. Particular attention is given to the incident of Indrajit's *Naga-astra,* the serpent-weapon (fig. 59).[3] After the final battle, Rama, Sita, whose fire ordeal is only mentioned in the caption, Lakshmana and the allies fly to Ayodhya in the *Pushpaka Vimana* (aerial chariot) and celebrate Rama's coronation.

The large central tableau displays the classic version of the *Ramapattabhisheka.*

Large borders with floral—in this case, lotus design—or geometric patterns are characteristic of the Kalahasti *kalamaris.* Generally a chevron pattern is used between individual scenes. Festoons and hangings appear consistently on the upper part of the panel. They probably have the same purpose as punctuation in a written text: they define the various phases of the action.

Compared to the brilliant palette of the Coastal Andhra *Ramayanas,* the works of the Srikalahasti atelier, with their limited range of hues, seem rather monotonous. A concise characterization of the human figures appearing in the Srikalahasti *kalmkaris* has been offered by Irwin and Hall: "The characters are stock types, drawn from a set of stencils of highly formalised poses and *mudras* from Indian dance and drama. Each stencil may be used for all the similar characters in a given situation, the only variation being in the colour and pattern of the costume. As many of these details are applied by the mordant painter after the master-artist has completed his outline, they are often quite arbitrary, and identification of individual persons may be difficult without close knowledge of the story".[4]

The scenes are set in either a landscape—suggested by trees or plants imaginatively rendered—or in a hall. Among the former, the seascapes are noteworthy (e.g. no. 56). The palaces consist of two columns supporting a roof occasionally adorned by merlons (e.g. no. 35). There are exceptions to this stark simplicity: the cityscapes with their domes and spires (e.g. nos. 26, 49), and the sumptuous central tableau.

Ramayana Srikalahasti

CAPTIONS

Balakanda

1. *Before starting to write the Srimad Ramayana, prayers, bananas, coconuts, different kinds of food items, betel leaves were offered to Vinayaka [Ganesha], and he [the artist] prostrated himself at the feet of the deity and prayed that with his blessings and without any interruption he could write the Ramayana.*

2. *While Vishnu was lying on his snake bed in Vaikuntha, Brahma, Indra, Agni, Varuna, Vayu, Kubera, Ishana, the eight dikpalas, cows, Chitrasena gandharva, Tumburu, Narada, Yaksha, Paksha, Naga, the eleven Rudras, all of them came to him. They requested his help because they were tormented by Ravana and*

Kumbhakarna. He heard their plea and promised that he would be born in the house of Dashratha maharaja and would sort out their difficulties. Having heard this, the devatas were very happy and retired.

3. *Narada arrives at Valmiki's anthill and announces that he [Valmiki] will compose the Ramayana, and then [Narada] returns happily to Vaikuntha [Vishnu's celestial abode].*

4. *All the elders came together at the court of Romapada maharaja to discuss the drought afflicting the country, and how to overcome this problem. Then he [the ascetic] said that there was a person in Madhuvana,⁵ Rishyashringa, [who could help] and should be invited.*

5. *Romapada maharaja and the elders summoned the beautiful courtesans, instructed them to go Madhuvana where Rishyashringa lived, and to bring him back with them. So the courtesans departed happily.*

6. *The courtesans arrived in Madhuvana, looked around and found Rishyashringa. They offered him tasty food, played with him, dallied with him and he fell for them. Eventually, he left with them.*

7. *The courtesans carried him in a palanquin to Romapada maharaja's country. The king came to welcome Rishyashringa, bade him to sit on a bejewelled lion throne and performed puja namaskaram. Immediately the whole place brightened up.*

8. *On an auspicious day, Romapada maharaja married his daughter Shanta to Rishyashringa. Instruments were played, everybody rejoiced and the couple was blessed with sanctified rice.*

9. *Dasharatha maharaja, Vasishtha, Rishyashringa and other dignitaries were all present at the ashvamedha yaga. The horse was worshipped, abundantly fed and let loose. It roamed through many countries, came back where it started and stood still, facing towards north. This made everybody happy.* (fig. 9)

Fig. 9

10. *Dasharatha maharaja, Vasishtha, Rishyashringa and other elders performed the putrakameshti yaga. Then Prajapati came out from the yaga and gave Dasharatha the payasa [sweet] saying: "You should give this to your three wives, Sumitra and others". Then he took the payasa and returned to his palace.*

    Although this and the previous caption mention Rishyashringa, the sage is not shown.

11. *Dasharatha brings the payasa. He summons his three wives to the inner chamber. Before taking the payasa they bathed, and then, he gave them the sweet one by one. They partook of it with great respect. He blessed them and wishes them every success.*

12. *Different portions of Narayana incarnated into their wombs, they grew day by day and, at an auspicious time, they were born to Kausalya, Sumitra and Kaikeyi. They were overjoyed and happily singing lullabies.*

13. *Dasharatha maharaja consults Vasishtha and requests him to name the babies: Sri Rama, Lakshmana, Bharata, Shatrughna.*

14. *King Dasharatha requests Vasishtha to teach [his sons] writing, the fourteen Puranas, all the Vedas, and all the Granthas [holy scriptures]. He teaches them all the arts and educates them. They prostrate in front of Vasishtha, he blesses them, and they rejoice.*

15. *At the request of Dasharatha maharaja, Vasishtha, apart from these subjects, instructs Sri Rama, Bharata, Lakshmana and Shatrughna, also in the use of the Agni-astra, Brahma-astra and Vayu-astra [different types of magical weapons]. They became experts in the use of these weapons and everybody was surprised to see their extraordinary skills. They blessed them wishing them every success in their lives.*

16. *While Dasharatha maharaja, Sri Rama, Lakshmana, Bharata and Shatrughna were in the assembly hall, Vishvamitra arrived and requested the king to let his sons accompany him. He [Dasharatha] said "They are still very young"; at this Vishvamitra gets angry.*

17. *Vishvamitra takes Sri Rama and Lakshmana with him. As they were walking, he spoke to them about the various sacred rivers, in particular about the Ganga. While they were crossing it, Tataki, a rakashasi, appeared before them. Sri Rama asked Vishvamitra: "Who is this?" Vishvamitra replies: "She is Tataki, a rakshasi". As soon as he said this, Sri Rama immediately killed her and was blessed by Vishvamitra who wished him every success.*

    Rama, Lakshmana, and Vishvamitra on their way to the forest are accompanied by Dasharatha. The sage points to a river, the Ganga, towards which they resolutely proceed. The crossing of the river symbolizes a new phase of life for the youths: the king disappears, and Rama performs his first heroic act by killing the dark-complexioned *rakshasi* Tataki, who, armed with an uprooted tree, rushes towards them.

18. *While he [Sri Rama] was walking, his feet touched a stone. Ahalya, who was transformed into a stone, came to life and said: "My curse is removed thanks to you", and then she greeted Rama with folded hands. Victory to Sri Rama.*

19. *While they were walking, Janaka maharaja came to meet them and took them to his palace. Once they were in his palace, he talked to them and wished them every success.*

20. *While they were walking, Janaka maharaja asked: "Who are these good people?" Vishvamitra said, "They are the sons of Dasharatha maharaja and they come to see Shiva's bow". When he said this, Janaka maharaja asked Shiva's bow to be brought. As soon as it was brought, Sri Rama broke it into two. Seeing this, all the other kings and ministers were surprised.*

21. *Janaka maharaja writes a letter to Dasharatha maharaja and sends it to him.*

22. *The letter is handed to Dasharatha maharaja. He reads it, rejoices and replies. The messenger departs happily.*

23. *Dasharatha maharaja and his wives, Kaikeyi, Kausalya and Sumitra ride on a chariot and arrive at Janaka maharaja's country. Victory to Sri Rama.*

A chariot, oddly enough, depicted without wheels but drawn by a diminutive horse, carries the three queens to Mithila. The speed of this cumbersome conveyance is suggested by a fluttering flag fixed on its eave. A guard shows the way to Dasharatha's capital.

24. *On an auspicious day, Janaka maharaja marries his daughter Sitadevi to Sri Rama, Urmila to Lakshmana, Malavika to Bharata, Shrutakirti to Shatrughna. All the various instruments were played, mantras were chanted, everybody sprinkled yellow rice, and the sumangalis were singing songs. The apsaras Urvashi, Menaka, Tilottama, danced. With all this, the wedding was celebrated in a grand manner.*

Although the caption enumerates four weddings, the artist has shown only three.

Ayodhyakanda

25. *Dasharatha maharaja and his ministers sat in court. They called Sri Rama and Sitadevi and told them: "Tomorrow we are going to celebrate the royal coronation". Both of them rejoiced. Victory to Sri Rama.*

26. *Manthara watches from upstairs. She comes down to Kaikeyi and informs her that Sri Rama's royal coronation was to be celebrated on the following day. Manthara tells her: "You should get now the three favours he [Dasharatha] promised you".* (fig. 26)

This scene is divided into two. The vignette to the left depicts the moment in which Manthara discovers the plans for Rama's imminent coronation. She looks down from a rooftop terrace—noteworthy is the rendering of the cityscape—and, without losing a moment, rushes to warn Kaikeyi of the imminent ceremony.[6] To the right, she stands opposite queen Kaikeyi who listens to her. In Manthara's hand is a necklace (?), a present from the queen.

Fig. 26

27. *Kaikeyi lowers her veil and looks disconsolate. Dasharatha maharaja holds her hand and takes her into the room. She asks him to fulfil his three promises.*

28. *Kaikeyi summons Sri Rama and Sita. She tells them that Dasharatha maharaja has fulfilled her wishes and tells them to go to the forest for fourteen years; she gives them ochre robes and sends them away.*

The dejected king, on the verge of swooning, sits behind Kaikeyi who looks unperturbed. The ochre robes mentioned in the caption indicate that from now on Rama and Sita will lose their royal status and become homeless wanderers. The *jatas*, matted hair, mentioned in no. 30 are yet another external sign of their loss of status.

29. *Sri Rama, Lakshmana and Sita request the chariot to be ready for their departure.*

Although the text refers to Lakshmana and a chariot, these are not shown.

30. *Sri Rama, Lakshmana and Sita, the three of them, arrived to Guha's ashrama. They sat under a tree; their hair was tied in jatas. Guha came to meet them, did pada puja to Sri Rama and prostrated himself before him. After he did all this, Rama gave him salvation and Guha rejoiced.*

Conforming to their exile status, Rama, Lakshmana and Sita wear their matted hair tied in a topknot. Striking is the tree shown with two crowns, one shading Rama, the other Lakshmana (see also no. 40).

Aranyakanda

31. *While Sri Rama, Sita and Lakshmana, the three of them, were in the Dandakaranya, Shurpanakha came, and fell in love with Sri Rama. Lakshmanasvami cut off her ears and nose.*

32. *Shurpanakha ran to her brothers Khara, Doshana, Trisharadu saying that Sri Rama and Lakshmana have insulted her. On hearing this, they got angry: "We are going to kill whoever did this, this very second!" Having said this they set off on their journey.*

33. *Khara, Doshana and others, accompanied by the whole army and by the band [playing] battle bugles and drums, marched against Sri Rama and Lakshmana.*

As noted above (no. 23) the conveyances, drawn by diminutive horses, are devoid of wheels.

34. *Sri Rama saw Khara, Doshana, Trisharadu and the whole of their fierce army coming towards him. He requested Lakshmana to look after Sitadevi while he went to fight against the rakshasas, whom he annihilated in one minute. Victory to Sri Rama!*

35. *While Sri Rama, Lakshmana and Sitadevi were in the hut, Maricha comes in the form of a deer. Looking at it, Sitadevi asks Rama to catch it for her. Sri Rama pursues that deer, shoots arrows at it and it falls dead.*

36. *Ravana, in disguise, arrives at the hut and asks for bhiksha* [alms]. *Sitadevi brings some bhiksha and stands on the threshold.*

At the extreme right, Ravana appears in all his majesty: ten-headed and twenty-armed, armed with a large trident.

37. *Ravana abducted Sitadevi and while his aerial chariot was travelling through the sky, Jatayu obstructs its way and fights* [against Ravana] *fiercely. Ravana, however, cuts Jatayu's wings off and he, barely breathing, falls down to earth.*

An alcove with a large bolster, on the left, symbolizes the empty hut.

38. *Rama and Lakshmana searched for Sitadevi in the hut. When they discover that she was missing they were devastated.*

39. *While Sri Rama and Lakshmana searched for Sitadevi, they came across Jatayu, who was just on the verge of breathing his last. He, however, told them about Sitadevi in detail.*

Rama carries in his outstretched hand Jatayu's body engulfed in a blazing flame.[7]

Kishkindhakanda

40. *Searching for Sitadevi, Sri Rama and Lakshmana arrived near a lake. While they were doing their morning rituals, Hanuman came to greet Sri Rama in a friendly manner.*

41. *During their search for Sita, Sri Rama and Lakshmana met Sugriva and Hanuman, who gave them the bag containing Sitadevi's jewellery. When Sri Rama looked at it, he felt very sad.*

42. *Sugriva, beaten by Vali, came to Sri Rama* [for help]. *Sri Rama asks Lakshmanasvami to put a garland of flowers around his neck. Lakshmanasvami obeys and does so.*

43. *After having spoken to Sri Rama and Lakshmana, Sugriva, with a garland around his neck, roaring, returns to Kishkindha. Vali looks at him and senses that he has yet again come to fight against him. While they fight fiercely, Sri Rama hides behind a tree and shoots an arrow at Vali. The latter falls to the ground and dies.*

When Rama's arrow hits Vali, he falls backwards, dying, into Tara's arms. Behind her is an attendant who raises her hands in distress. (This figure has been repaired with a piece of an old *kalamkari*.)

44. *When Vali died, Tara and Angada* [Vali's son] *were distressed. They took him, performed the funeral rites and felt very sad.*

45. *On Sri Rama's advice, Lakshmana crowns Sugriva and proclaims him king, while Angada becomes the heir apparent. On that occasion the musical instruments were played and everybody rejoiced.*

46. *Hanuman, Jambavan, and other monkey-courtiers were at Sugriva's and Angada's court. He* [Sugriva] *summons all the vanaras* [monkeys] *tells them to go in all the four sides* [i.e. directions] *in search of Sitadevi, and bring her back as soon as possible. They happily start on their journey.*

47. *Sri Rama and Lakshmana call Hanuman. Sri Rama entrusts to him his signet ring, and asks him to find the whereabouts of Sitadevi. Hanuman takes the ring, and with their blessings starts his journey.*

Sundarakanda

48. *Hanuman took up the appearance of a very small creature and he jumped over the ocean.*

49. *Hanuman, as a small creature, enters the kingdom of Lanka, catches Lankini by the hair, easily beats the life out of her, and proceeds further.* (fig. 49)

Fig. 49

Once in Lanka, Hanuman tries to find an opening through which to enter the city. He sees a huge gate but it is closed. He demolishes it, and is confronted by a huge dark-skinned woman armed with a trident, who blocks the entrance. Undeterred, he punches and kicks the life out of her. She is the tutelary deity of Lanka, who in her previous birth was Vijayalakshmi, the guard of Brahma's treasury. Once, however, she failed her duties and was cursed to reborn as Lankalakshmi, i.e. Lankini. She was told that she would be freed from her curse, on being struck down by Hanuman's blows. The city is suggested by two buildings with a spire-like superstructure, surrounded by a crenellated enclosure wall. In it, two guards with goat's heads, raise their arms in distress at the sight of Lankini's demise.

50. *Hanuman arrives into the Ashokavana, looks everywhere, spots Sitadevi, shows her the signet ring and reveals himself to her in his real form. Sitadevi entrusts him with the chudamani jewel.*

After meeting Sita, Hanuman assumes his formidable aspect; huge and with bared fangs, he is ready to wreck Ravana's *Ashokavana*.

51. *Hanuman in the Ashokavana fiercely attacks the rakshasas and kills them. Frightened, they run to Ravana reporting that a monkey has entered the garden killing the rakshasas. Ravana says to Indrajit: "You go and catch him".*

52. *Indrajit captures Hanuman and drags him before Ravana. Hanuman sits before Ravana who asks him angrily: "How could you come past the seven seas?" And Hanuman replies: "This is only a canal for me, so I came swimming." At this, Ravana decides to kill him, and summons Vibhishana to do the job.*

53. *On Ravana's order they tied clothes to his* [Hanuman's] *tail and set fire to them. Hanuman, however, set fire to the town, except for Vibhishana's house, and easily escaped from them.*[8]

54. *After burning the whole of Lanka, Hanuman cools his tail in the ocean.*

    The layout of this scene is similar to no. 48. The speed of the flight is suggested by Hanuman's billowing *angavastra*.

55. *He arrives at the presence of Sri Rama and Lakshmana and tells them whereabouts of Sitadevi, as well as how he 'insulted Lanka'* [i.e. how he destroyed Lanka].

Yuddhakanda

56. *Sri Rama and Lakshmana called Vibhishana and said that a bridge had to be built. At that time Vibhishana was at the orders of Sri Rama and Lakshmana. He was helped by Hanumanta* [Hanuman], *Angada, Nala, Nila, Jambavan as well as by other vanaras who collected rocks and trees. Using the trees, they built a raft of one-hundred yojanas* [approximately one-thousand miles] *in length, and with an army of seven-thousand vanaras they travelled to Lanka.*[9] (fig. 56)

Fig. 56

57. *Sri Rama calls Angada and asks him to tell Ravana to surrender: "If you surrender you will live, if not we will destroy you and your relatives". Angada takes this message and starts the journey.*

58. *Angada goes to Ravana and says: "You surrender and give up Sitadevi, otherwise your friends, relatives and others will be killed". He spoke to him rudely.* (fig. 58)

Fig. 58

Before the war actually begins, Rama sends Angada on a diplomatic mission to Ravana with a view to persuade him to return Sita. Although it looks as if Angada is on the verge of kicking Ravana's crown off—this happens at a later stage—this scene may refer to the following story: Once at Ravana's court and seeing that words would not persuade him, Angada planted his foot firmly on the ground, and challenged those who were present to uproot his foot. If anybody were to accept the challenge and was successful, Rama would concede defeat and return without Sita. Although all the *rakshasa* commanders and even Indrajit tried to lift Angada's leg, none succeeded. Ravana, humiliated by this failure, slowly walked towards Angada's planted foot and just as he was about to hold Angada's leg to attempt the challenge, Angada moved away and Ravana fell down.

59. *Both Sri Rama and Lakshmana were unconscious because of Indrajit's snake-arrows. Then Narada arrived and prayed to Lord Garudasvami, asking that they may be revived. Thus, Garudasvami revived them, woke them up and they started their journey [?]. Victory to Sri Rama!* (fig. 59)

Fig. 59

This episode is popular with the Kalahasti artists. The version of the incident illustrated here is inspired by the *Ranganatha Ramayana*'s narrative. Narada comes to the battlefield to inform Rama that only Garuda's intervention can save the situation. Garuda is the natural enemy of the snakes, and his appearance on the battlefield restores the fallen princes to health.[10]

60. *Sri Rama and Lakshmanasvami wake up. The latter shoots the Agni-astra on Indrajit and kills him. Sri Rama shoots his Brahma-astra on Kumbhakarna* [and kills him] *while the vanaras are fiercely fighting against the rakshasas, killing them. Victory to Sri Rama.*

61. *Sri Rama and Ravana are fighting violently and Sri Rama disperses Ravana's army, Ravana's chariot is broken, his elephant killed. He cuts off Ravana's heads, he shoots an arrow at his stomach where the amrita kalasha was kept, thus killing him. Victory to Sri Rama!*

62. *Sri Rama, Lakshmanasvami, Sitadevi and Vibhishana travel to Ayodhya in the Pushpaka Vimana. Victory to Sri Rama!*

Ramapattabhisheka

63. *Sri Rama, Lakshmanasvami, Sitadevi went to the forest. They killed Ravana, Kumbhakarna, Indrajit, Maharakshasas, Virupaksha, Vyashaka, Prahasta, Adikaya, Mahakaya, Shumba, Nishumba, Shumbakeshaya—all of them were destroyed.*

Then, Sitadevi, the very faithful wife, was forced to go into the fire [i.e. undergo the fire ordeal]. *Vasishtha* [?]. *Ganga, Yamuna, Sarasvati, Godavari, Narmada, Sindhu, Kaveri—all these sacred rivers came to lustrate Sri Rama. He then sat on the throne embossed with precious stones, and on which was spread the skin of a lion. He was adorned with precious jewels. The gandharvas were singing, Tumburu and Narada played the vina, Lakshmana waved the fly-whisk, Bharata held the umbrella and Shatrughna stood at his side. The apsaras Rambha, Urvashi and Tilottama, danced. All the Brahmins threw akshate. In the midst of all this, Sri Rama was crowned and sat happily on the throne while everybody wished him every success.*

Notes

1. Other examples of this style are: the *Ramayana* with English captions (cat. 4) and *The Life of Christ* (cat. 19) in the present collection; the *Virata Parvan* (Asia 1991,0327,0.1); the *Ramayana* (Asia As1966,01.496; see below) and the *Mahabharata* (Asia As1966,01.497; see p. 11) in the collection of the British Museum. For a detailed discussion of these hangings, see Dallapiccola 2010: 252–258; 264–270; 270–277. Further examples of hangings from this area are in the Ashmolean Museum, Oxford (Harle and Topsfield 1987:69–70) and in the Calico Museum of Textiles, Ahmedabad (Irvin and Hall 1971: 66–67, 78–79, pl. 43).

2. The *Ramayana* (Asia As1966,01.496) in the collection of the British Museum (see below). See also Dallapiccola 2010: 274–270. This episode is illustrated on p. 268, cat. no. 31.6.3.

3. *Ramayana* (cat. 4) and Dallapiccola 2010: 265, cat. no. 31.7.3.

4. Irwin and Hall 1971: 75.

5. In the Valmikian and other narrative traditions Madhuvanam is the grove where the *vanaras* celebrated the return of Hanuman from Lanka after discovering Sita. In the Srikalahasti works, it is the forest in which Rishyashringa lives.

6. Her animosity against Rama goes back to the time when the young prince, while playing with a stick, hit her leg breaking it. This story is given in the 14th-century Telugu *Ranganatha Ramayana* (Sarma 1973: 81).

7. This convention is noted in a number of other *kalamkaris* from Andhra (see cat. 1.45, cat. 1, n. 16, and cat. 2.49).

8. The layout of this scene recalls that of the *Ramayana* (Asia As1966,01.496) in the collection of the British Museum. (see below). See also Dallapiccola 2010: 268–269, cat. no. 31.5.2.

9. The layout of this scene recalls that of the *Ramayana* (Asia As1966, 01.496) in the collection of the British Museum (see below). See also in Dallapiccola 2010: 268–269, cat. no. 31.6.2.

10. The layout of this scene recalls that of the *Ramayana* (Asia As1966,01.496) in the collection of the British Museum (see below). See also Dallapiccola 2010: 268–269, cat. no. 31.7.3.

Ramayana from Srikalahasti, British Museum, Asia As1966,01.496

Ramayana SRIKALAHASTI
English Captions

4

Ramayana Srikalahasti (English Captions)

The object history note reveals that this cloth was bought by the Second Lieutenant Henry Castree Hughes from "a village consisting of three temples, some good craft shops and little else" in 1915. The name of the village is not recorded.[1] There can be no doubt about the provenance of this item, as it displays all the stylistic and iconographic features typical of the Srikalahasti area workshops.[2] The sketchy description of the place, "three temples, some good crafts shops…" may suggest that the cloth was, in fact, bought at or near Srikalahasti, whose Kalahastishvara temple complex and smaller shrines on the neighbouring hills, dominate the town.

Although the workmanship is rather crude this cloth is exceptional in that it has English captions written in a good hand by a local person with a fairly good command of English.

One wonders whether this hanging was commissioned by a British person, or if such items were routinely produced to be sold to foreign visitors, as was the case with albums depicting Indian trades, castes, customs, etc. Another peculiarity of this work is that the narrative is incomplete. As usual in the works of the Srikalahasti area, the captions are more informative than the illustrations.

The story is laid out in eight rows accommodated around the central tableau displaying the *Ramapattabhisheka*, Rama's coronation. In the first row the artist has arranged the preliminaries of the story, beginning with the Ganesha *puja*, the gods imploring Vishnu to descend to earth, and Narada discovering Valmiki in the anthill (fig. 3). This is followed by a detailed rendering of the story of Dasharatha's accidental killing of the young ascetic, Guruputra (fig. 4).[3]

---

4. Ramayana from Srikalahasti
IS 5-1977
Dimensions: 270 x 252 cm
Date: early 20th century (?)
Provenance: Srikalahasti area
Captions: in English, written by a local English speaker

The story of the drought in the Anga kingdom, followed by all the incidents leading to Rishyashringa's wedding with Shanta, Dasharatha's *putrakameshti yaga* and the birth of the four princes come next.

The narrative then jumps from the princes' naming ceremony to Rama, Sita and Lakshmana being banished to the forest (fig.15).

The episode of the golden deer is shown in detail while Sita's abduction and the death of Jatayu do not appear. The narrative resumes with the arrival of the princes in Kishkindha (fig. 17). Dispensing with the stories of Vali and Sugriva's rivalry, the narrative picks up again at Hanuman's crossing the ocean and his meeting with Sita. The burning of Lanka is mentioned in passing in the caption. The last scene on the cloth is mysterious: it shows Ravana departing as if in a huff (fig. 19), leaving the narrative incomplete. Not only the various battles described in the *Yuddhakanda* have been ignored, but even the final encounter between Rama and Ravana has not been illustrated. The caption above the *Ramapattabhisheka* informs the viewer of the successful outcome of the Lanka expedition and of the return of the exiles and their allies to Ayodhya where Rama's coronation is celebrated with the usual pomp and circumstance.

The border of the cloth is constituted by motifs, typical of the Srikalahasti master dyers: the outermost is a thin *pilli adugu* [cat's footsteps] motif, then a broader cartwheel pattern and, finally, the *pilli adugu* is repeated. The same scheme is repeated around the central tableau, only that in this case, between the two *pilli adugu* borders, there is a chevron pattern. The division between the scenes are summarily indicated by a double line, sometimes enlivened by a crude decorative motif.

Ramayana Srikalahasti (English Captions)

CAPTIONS

Balakanda

1. *To write the history of Sreemattu Ramayanum prayers should be offered to Vigneswara* [Ganesha] *before commencing so as to succeeded* [sic] *from beginning to the end.*

2. *Then Swamy* [Vishnu] *was sleaping* [sic] *on a snake (Seshasayanum) at Vaikuntum. Sreedevi Niladevi Budevi* [sic] *and some others while pressing the feat* [sic] *Brahma Indra Agni Yama Nairutti Varuna Vayuvaya Kubera Esaniya and other Dikpalakas and Sanathkumaras & others came & complained before Swamy that they are very much troubled by Ravana.*

   Only few of the deities mentioned in the caption are shown here. Vishnu reclines on the five-headed serpent Shesha—hence his epithet Sheshashayana—behind which stands Garuda. Sridevi, Niladevi, and Bhudevi, the deity's three consorts, are seated at his feet. Bhudevi's head is turned towards a delegation of celestials: the four-headed Brahma followed by Indra, Vayu, and Kubera, three *dikpalas*.

3. *Naratha went to the place where Valmiki and other sages were, and informed them that in the next birth, Swamy would incarnate himself as Sreerama.* (fig. 3)

   Fig. 3

   The text suggests that Valmiki was living in an *ashrama*. The artist, however, following the traditional narrative, shows his head emerging out of a schematically rendered anthill covered by trees and bushes. Narada, with the *vina* resting on his shoulder, approaches him.

4. *One Guruputra (Son of a Sage) was carring* [sic] *his parents in a balance on his shoulders to Banaris* [sic]. *When they came near this tank his parents asked him to get some water to drink.* (fig. 4)

   Fig. 4

Ramayana Srikalahasti (English Captions)

5. *He hung the balance* [i.e. the yoke] *to a tree & went to tank with a vesavl* [vessel] *to get water. While he was dipping the vasael* [vessel] *into the water Dasaratha heard the noise of bubbles.*

6. *Thasaratha* [sic] *shot Guruputra arrow* [sic] *thinking that an elephant has come to drink water.*

7. *Dasaratha told to the parents of Guruputra that he has killed their son thinking him to be an elephant. They* [illegible] *that Dasaratha also may dies* [sic] *by leaving* [illegible].

8. *In the kingdom of Romapathamaharaju there was a terrible famine. He asked some sages about it. They replied that one Rushyasringa* [sic].

9. *Then the dancing girals* [sic] *went to Maduvanum*[4] *Rushaya* [sic] *Srunga ran away. The dancing girals followed him nakedly and reached Rushya* [sic] *Srunga.*

This incident illustrated elsewhere in great detail is reduced here to two vignettes.[5]

10. *Then the dancing girals* [sic] *tied a cloth to him and were carrying him in a palanquin into the kingdom.*[6]

11. *Romapatha* [sic] *maharaja gave his daughter Santadevi to him* [i.e. Rishyashringa] *in marriage with jewels and cloths. Dasaratha takes Rusha* [sic] *Srunga to Audiah* [Ayodhya].[7]

12. *Then Dasarada* [sic] *made an Asvamadayagam with several sages the horse goes and again comes to Eagnasala* [yajnashala] *after wandering several...* [illegible]

While the caption pointedly refers to the *ashvamedha* [horse sacrifice], the scene depicts the *putrakameshti yaga* [ritual to ensure the birth of a son]. King Dasharatha receives from the hands of the two-headed Agni the cup with the *payasa* [sweet]. To the extreme left, Rishyashringa, here again with a deer head, watches on.[8]

13. *Dasarada 3 wives ate payasam & delivered 4 male children at a good lagnam. After 10 days Dasarada saw his sons &* [was] *full joy.*

14. *Dasarada tried for the denomination of his sons Vasista. Valmiku* [sic]. *Narada. Kanva Baradvaya Visvamitra & others denominated and named them Sree Rama Lakshmana.*[9]

Ayodhyakanda

15. *Kaika* [Kaikeyi] *asked Dasarada to du* [sic] *coronation to her son as he promised before and to send Rama Lakshmana and Seetha to Asramum.* (fig. 15)

At the centre of the scene, Kaikeyi orders Rama and Sita to go the forest. According to the *Ranganatha Ramayana,* on hearing this, Dasharatha swoons (left). The queen holds in the hands the ochre cloths which the exiles will wear during their banishment.

Fig. 15

Aranyakanda

16. *Maricha went to... [illegible] river bank and where Seetha asked Rama to get her the deer went into the forest Rama ran behind it and at last Rama shot it with an arrow and the deer cried Lakshmana and this was heard by Seetha.*[10]

Kishkindhakanda

17. *Sugreeva saw Rama & Lakshmana and gave the jewels of Seetha to Rama saying that Rama* [a slip of the pen: it should be Ravana] *was carrying Seetha to Sylane* [Ceylon] *and that Seetha dropped the jewels on Rushyamugam.* (fig. 17)

Fig. 17

Although the caption mentions Sugriva handing over to Rama the jewels which Sita dropped from Ravana's chariot during the flight to Lanka, the bag containing the jewels is not as clearly shown as in cat. 3.41.[11]

Sundarakanda

18. and 19. *Hanumanta crossed the sea and reached Ceylon and saw Seetha at the Ashokavanum and gave the ring and informed the well fare* [sic] *of Rama and Lakshmana burruned* [sic] *Sylon* [sic] *and return to Rama. After Vebheeshuna the brother of Rama advised his brother Ravana to returned Seetha* [illegible] *great* [illegible]. (fig. 19)

(18.) Hanuman, with his hands raised and looking over his shoulders towards the mainland, elegantly steps over the sea, depicted as a rushing stream filled with aquatic life.[12]

(19.) Hanuman meets Sita in the *Ashokavana*. He appears first in his diminutive and, eventually, in his usual form. Floating in the air between Sita, seated beneath the tree and Hanuman, is an object which could be her head-jewel, the *chudamani*.[13]

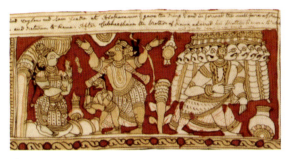

Fig. 19

The last scene of this *kalamkari* is mysterious: separated by a tree from the foregoing, it depicts the ten-headed and twenty-armed Ravana resolutely walking out of the picture. Possibly this scene may refer to Ravana's visit to Sita: he tries to persuade her to forget Rama and to accept his love if she wants Rama to be saved. She refuses and warns him that his end is fast approaching.

Central tableau

20. *Rama & Lakshmana & Seeta having gone to the forest then to Ceylon where they killed demons namely Ravana Kumbakarna Gudragitta Auttikaya Mahakaya Dumracha Virupaksa & others. Lastly they went in flower chariots to their city Avidiah. Rama having seated on the thrown* [sic] *having Seatha* [sic] *at his left foot and his beloved brother Lakshmana at his right and his other beloved brothers.*

Strangely enough, Shatrughna has been omitted from this tableau and, unusually, Bharata carries a fly-whisk instead of the umbrella.

Notes

1. V&A Registry, RP 77/64.
2. The layout and the iconography are based on the 'standard' Srikalahasti *Ramayana* hanging, e.g. cat. 3, but greatly simplified.
3. This episode has been omitted in cat. 3.
4. See cat. 3, n. 5.
5. E.g. the lengthy narrative in the canopies from Chirala (cat. 1.10) and Machilipatnam (cat. 2. 7, cat. 2.9–2.10). In the works from the Srikalahasti area this incident is not highlighted as in those from Coastal Andhra.
6. Similar iconography and layout in cat. 3.7.
7. Similar iconography and layout in cat. 3.8.
8. Here it is the two-headed Agni who emerges from the flames, handing the *payasa* over to the king, whereas in cat. 3.10, it is Prajapati.
9. Only the chief queen, Kausalya, attends the naming ceremony here, whereas in cat. 3.13, two queens are shown.
10. The caption refers to Maricha's cry for Lakshmana's help, imitating Rama's voice. On hearing it, Sita insists that Lakshmana should go to Rama's help, leaving her alone in the hut. Similar iconography and layout in cat. 3.35.
11. The jewellery is clearly depicted in cat. 2.50.
12. Similar iconography and layout in cat. 3.48.
13. The painter has omitted to show Hanuman perched on the tree beneath which sits Sita. See cat. 3.50.

Ramayana Sri Lanka

5

5 Ramayana Sri Lanka

**5. Ramayana from Sri Lanka
5440 (IS)**
Dimensions: 267 x 550 cm
Date: early 19th century
Provenance: Sri Lanka
Captions: in Tamil

This is the largest *kalamkari* of the present collection and, perhaps, one of the most interesting. Its layout is unusual as there is no central tableau and there are no divisions between scenes or episodes. The narrative surprisingly commences with the *Ayodhyakanda* and includes a number of rarely illustrated incidents: e.g. the story of Mayiliravana, 'Peacock Ravana', and a few scenes of *Uttarakanda*. The explanatory captions, which often are more informative than the illustrations, and the identifying labels, are in a 'corrupt' Tamil. Despite all the variations in the narrative, this work follows, by and large, the classic storyline.

All the figures bear small paper labels pasted on the textile, displaying a neatly written number. The previous owner had probably compiled a key, now unfortunately lost, to follow the intricate narrative. In the present volume the scenes have been grouped as shown on the guide on p. 83.

The top register shows a series of deities, perhaps inspired by the procession of deities, *dikpalas* and *rishis* imploring Vishnu to descend to earth, observed in the works from Andhra. There is, however, a crucial difference: here the gods and their consorts are not paying homage to Vishnu, but they are shown frontally; they ride on their animal conveyances, and some of them are flanked by *pujaris* worshipping them. Probably their purpose was to allow the viewer to have *darshana* and pay homage to them before viewing the *Ramayana* narrative.

The actual story commences in the second register. The *Ayodhyakanda* begins with a sequence of palace scenes introducing King Dasharatha and his family. The impending coronation of Rama is hinted at in no. 11, when Vasishtha talks to King Dasharatha. The next scene depicts the hunchback, Kuni, whispering something to Queen Sumitra. In this version of the narrative, Kuni is Sumitra's and not Kaikeyi's servant. Whether this is an error of the scribe or a local variation on the *Ramayana* story remains to be ascertained. There is an unexpected variation from the 'traditional' plot: when the exiles are ready to leave, Bharata and his followers try to prevent Rama from going to the forest (no. 14), but their attempt fails. This variation is significant, because with the intervention of Bharata at this point of the narrative, the meeting of the exiled Rama with his brothers on Mount Chitrakuta, one of the key episodes of the story, is omitted.

The *Aranyakanda* commences with the Shurpanakha episode (fig. 16). Here, Shurpanakha falls in love with Lakshmana, not with Rama. This unusual version of the story may be due to the conflation of two distinct episodes: the classic one in which Shurpanaka falls in love with Rama and is eventually mutilated by Lakshmana, and the less renowned one of the *rakshasi* Ayomukhi. The latter falls madly in love with Lakshmana but he does not reciprocate her sentiments.[1] In this case too, Lakshmana loses his patience and cuts her nose and breasts off.

Shurpanakha's mutilation causes Ravana to send three of his brothers to fight against Rama. While in the Machilipatnam canopy (cat. 2.47), following the Valmikian narrative, Lakshmana and Sita abscond in a cave for the duration of the conflict, here Lakshmana, instead of Rama, confronts and defeats Ravana's *rakshasas*. The narrative then resumes its traditional course with the episode of the golden gazelle, Sita's abduction, and the death of Jatayu shown here as a winged ascetic called Jatayumuni.

In the *Kishkindhakanda*, the episodes of Rama's felling of the seven palm trees[2] and of Vali's death are conflated (fig. 24). Skipping various episodes, the narrative moves quickly to the *Sundarakanda*. Hanuman jumps across the ocean (fig. 25) to Lanka and meets Sita. He then wrecks Ravana's garden and is taken captive by Indrajit. Once in Ravana's presence, incensed at the king's arrogance, Hanuman kicks off his crown (fig. 30).

The war begins: the episode of the building of the causeway is, strangely enough, ignored. Fearing Mayiliravana's (here called Malyavan)[3] magic arts, Vibhishana entrusts Hanuman to guard Rama and Lakshmana. Hanuman, suspecting some foul play, tries to protect them by surrounding their camp with his tail (fig. 33). They, however, are kidnapped by the *rakshasas* of Mayiliravana, spirited away and carried in a box to Patala Lanka, a subterranean kingdom beneath the ocean. They are to be sacrificed to the goddess Kali, but for the arrival of Hanuman who, at the eleventh hour finds out their whereabouts, frees them, and sacrifices Mayiliravana to the goddess (no. 33). Once back from Patala Lanka, Lakshmana confronts Indrajit, whose weapons are not strong enough against his prowess. Indrajit then resolves to use a magic weapon, the *nagapasha*, or snake-noose, which paralyzes the adversary. The *nagapasha* is imaginatively visualized as a large cobra encircling Lakshmana and his troops (no. 35). Eventually, Indrajit is killed. Then Kumbhakarna enters the scene and, in due course, the giant is decapitated by Lakshmana's arrow and not, as in most versions of the narrative, by Rama's. Lakshmana's leading role, which dramatically highlights Rama's aloofness, is one of the striking features of this *Ramayana*.

Lakshmana fights against Ravana and is wounded. Spirited away by Hanuman he is taken back to the camp where he lies on Rama's lap; this is Rama's first appearance on the battlefield after the Patala Lanka incident. Subsequently Hanuman flies to the Himalayas to fetch the miraculous herb, which restores Lakshmana's health (no. 42).

Only then Rama actively enters the fray and kills Ravana. Vibhishana is coronated king of Lanka, the exiles return to Ayodhya where they are welcomed by Bharata, and Rama's coronation is celebrated. This part of the narrative is very low key: there is no mention of either Sita's fire ordeal, or of Rama's and his allies' triumphal return to Ayodhya on the aerial chariot, the *Pushpaka Vimana.*

A few scenes of the *Uttarakanda* follow: Kusha and Lava, born after Sita is repudiated by Rama, wage war against him. The sage Valmiki narrates the story of their birth to Rama, he recognizes them, and the narrative ends on a happy note, with Rama, Sita and their sons seated on the throne.

A border with a floral design interspersed with diamond patterns frames the narrative. The background of the cloth is covered by a 'speckled' pattern, drawn very finely in black and highlighted with red: perhaps this pattern suggests the rain of flowers (*pushpavarsha*).[4]

Generally, the deities and the major characters of the story are represented in full-face view. From his banishment to the forest Rama is consistently shown four-armed, as if to stress his divine nature. Hanuman, Sugriva, Angada, Jambavan, Vibhishana, Indrajit and all other *vanaras* [monkeys] and *rakshasas* are shown either in profile or three-quarters profile.

The artist has devised different colour combinations for the various categories of characters.[5] Multiple-arms, e.g. Ravana's, are arranged as if either radiating from the elbow, or sprouting out of the upper arms of the main pair. The female figures' breasts are curiously drawn in such a way that they look like part of their necklaces.

The *mudras* are not differentiated, and the attributes are perfunctorily drawn and haphazardly placed. This leads one to suspect that the artists were not thoroughly familiar with the tenets of 'classical' iconography.

The numerous battle scenes not only display volleys of arrows in the background, but also rows of dismembered cadavers in the foreground (e.g. nos. 17, 34, 41). The scenes flow one into the other; however, occasionally they are divided by trees or birds. Buildings are suggested by lobed arches floating mid-air. Thrones are generally stepped and provided with bolsters and covered with patterned material. Particularly striking are the two scenes representing the ocean, both characterized by large aquatic animals and conch shells on a dark background. The trees, plants and animals are finely drawn.

5 Ramayana Sri Lanka

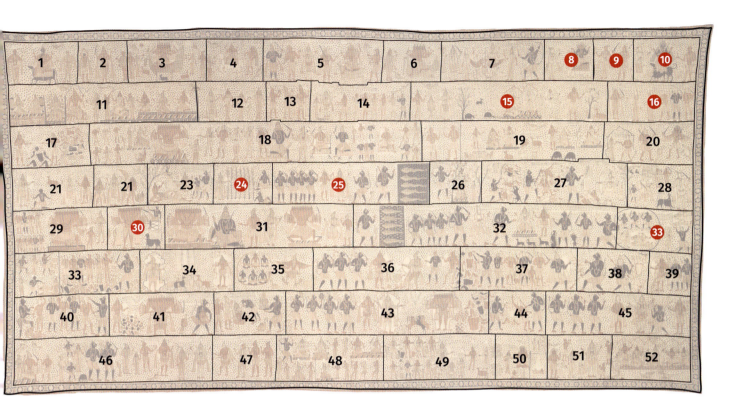

CAPTIONS

(Small paper labels bearing numbers, here in brackets, identify each figure.)

Deities

1. Worship of Vinayaka [Ganesha] (nos. 1–3)

    1. *Brahmin performing puja to Vinayaka*; 2. *Vinayaka riding on his bandicoot*; 3. *Brahmin showing the camphor lamp to Vinayaka.*

2. Daksha worships Virabhadra (nos. 4–6)

    4. *Daksha worships Virabhadrasvami*; 5. *Virabhadrasvami*; 6. *Attendant who holds an umbrella for Virabhadrasvami.*

3. Murugan, consorts, attendants, Surya and Chandra (nos. 7–13)

    7. *Attendant who holds an umbrella for Vallinasiki* [Vallinayaki]; 8. *Vallinasiki*; [not numbered] *Young deer*; 9. *Surya;*[6] 10. *Murugan sitting on a peacock*; 11. *Chandra*; 12. *Devanasiki* [Devanayaki] *Amman*; 13. *Person who holds the umbrella for Devanasiki Amman.*

4. Indra, Indrani and Narada (nos. 14–16)

14. Indrani; 15. Devendra on his elephant-vahana, Airavata; 16. Narada plays the vina at Indra's court.

5. Shiva's abode (nos. 17–22)

17. Demon-headed bhuta [goblin] who guards Shiva's abode; 18. Vyasa rishi; 19. Mahavishnu has come and stands before Shiva; 20. Nandi; 21. Paramashiva and Devi sitting together on the bull-vahana; 22. Attendant who holds the umbrella for Shiva.

6. Brahma and Sarasvati (nos. 23–24)

23. Sarasvati; 24. Brahma riding on the hamsa.

7. Vishnu's abode (nos. 25–29)

25. The guardian of Mahavishnu's gate; 26. Bhumidevi; 27. Mahavishnu sitting on Garuda;[7] *28. Mahalakshmi; 29. Hanuman.*[8]

8. Aiyanar and consorts (nos. 30–32) (fig. 8)

30. Purnai; 31. Aiyanar riding his elephant vahana; 32. Pudagalai.

Aiyanar, whose name means 'lord' or 'master', is the guardian deity and protector of the villages in Tamil Nadu. He rides on his four-tusked elephant and is flanked by his consorts Purnai and Pudagalai. Vira Mahakala is one of the guardians of Shiva's abode, and Bhairava is the fierce manifestation of Shiva's destructive power. These three deities are widely worshipped in rural areas of southern India.

Fig. 8

Fig. 9

9. Vira Mahakala (no. 33) (fig. 9)

33. Vira Mahakala.

He stands brandishing a sword in his right and a club in his left hand.

10. Worship of Bhairava (nos. 34–36) (fig. 10)

34. Brahmin performing puja to Bhairava; 35. Bhairavasvami with his dog-vahana; 36. Bhairava's servant.

Fig. 10

Black-complexioned Bhairava stands before his caparisoned and bejewelled black dog. On his dark forehead, both, the *tripundra* (horizontal marks worn by the devotees of Shiva) and the third eye stand out dramatically. He carries a trident and axe in his upper hands, a club and a sword in his lower ones. The two formally almost identical worship scenes at the beginning and at the end of this register, clearly define the space allotted to the deities.

Ayodhyakanda

11. Courtly intrigues (nos. 37–47)

    37. *Rama*; 38. *Sita*; 39. *Kaikesi* [Kaikeyi]; 40. *Deyatara* [Dasharatha]; 41. *[no caption]*; 42. *Bearer with a yak-tail fly-whisk*; 43. *Simittirai* [Sumitra]; 44. *Kuni* [Manthara]; 45. *Lakshmana*; 46. *Bharata*; 47. *Satturukkan* [Shatrughna].

    This first tableau introduces the main characters of the narrative. Rama and Sita seated in a hall; Kaikeyi, with a lotus flower in her left hand and a parrot perched on her right shoulder, sits on a throne near King Dasharatha. He discusses Rama's impending coronation with *rishi* Vasishtha.

    A female fly-whisk bearer stands at the side of Queen Sumitra seated on a throne; to her left is her hunchback servant Kuni.[9] The final part of this sequence depicts Rama's three brothers, seated, looking towards the queen and the plotting Kuni, awaiting in suspense the outcome of their deliberations.

12. The banishment (nos. 48–49)

    48. *Rama*; 49. *Kaikesi tells Rama to go to the forest.*[10]

13. The exiles take leave of the queens (nos. 50–55)

    50. *Sita*; 51. *Sita takes leave of Simittirai and Kaikesi before going to the forest.*[11] *Simittirai*; 52–53. *Rama, Sita and Lakshmana are banished*; 54. *Lakshmana accompanies them.*

14. Departure from Ayodhya (nos. 55–62)

    55. *Rama and Sita board the chariot to go to the forest*; 56–58. *Sita, Lakshmana and Rama are leaving, and Bharata*[12] *addresses him saying: "Brother, do not leave!"*

Rama answers: "In twelve years I will come back"[13] *and takes leave;*
59–60. Bharata's followers; 61–62. [no captions].

Aranyakanda

15. Life in the forest (nos. 63–71) (fig. 15)

    63. *Lakshmana;* 64. *Sita;* 65. *Rama arrives in the forest;* 66. *This is a forest with trees and birds;* 67–68. *Rama and Sita in the forest;* 69. *[no caption];* 70–71. *Lakshmana collects fruits and tubers for cooking.*

Fig. 15

16. The mutilation of Shurpanakha (nos. 72–75) (fig. 16)

    72. *[no caption];* 73. *Shurpanakha. When Shurpanakha sees Lakshmana she asks him to marry her, but he cuts her nose and her breasts;* 74–75. *Shurpanakha arrives crying and having seen her* [in this state] *the guards went to Ravana and reported. Ravana said that the person* [who did this] *should be persecuted and that he would go to fight against him.* [Near Shurpanakha:] *Guards at the door.*

Fig. 16

This is the sole hanging among those studied, in which Shurpanakha makes advances to Lakshmana. Lakshmana, brandishing a sword in his left hand, stands before Shurpanakha, whose nose and half of the right breast have been cut. There is no suggestion of Shurpanakha's visit to Rama's hut, or a depiction of Lakshmana jumping on her and mutilating her. The artist depicts the *fait accompli*.

17. Lakshmana fights against the *rakshasas* (nos. 76–79)

    76: *Lakshmana;* 77. *The guards have come to attack the man who cut Shurpanakha's nose;* 78. *A rakshasa;* 79. *All the rakshasas are killed.*

18. Ravana's court (nos. 80–88)

    80. *Rakshasas;* 81. *Fly-whisk bearer;* 82. *Ravana's wife;* 83. *Ravanan seated on his throne;* 84–85. *Shurpanakha cries saying that a human being has cut her nose*

and breasts. The guards tell him [Ravana] *that this human being lives with a woman and another man*; 86. *Guards*; 87. *Shurpanakha comes in crying with her nose and breasts cut off*; 88. [no caption].

Kumbhakarna and Indrajit (nos. 89–96)

89. [no caption]; 90. *Kumbhakarna*; 91. *A rakshasa*; 92–93. *Indrajit and his younger brother*; 94–96. *Indrajit and his army.*

Two of the main characters of the narrative are introduced here: Ravana's brother Kumbhakarna and Ravana's son Indrajit. Kumbhakarna, recognizable by his large dark body sits on a throne, flanked by armed *rakshasas*. Next to him are Indrajit and his younger brother. In the next scene, Indrajit, flanked by his bodyguards, imparts orders to a group of four *rakshasas*.

19. The golden deer (nos. 97–105)

97. *Ravana, having disguised himself as an ascetic* [with a view] *to abduct Sita, requests Maricha to lure Rama away*; 98. *Maricha*; 99. *Lakshmana*; 100. *Sita*; 101. *Rama*; 102. *Maricha, in the guise of a deer, arrives and plays around*; 103. *Sita asks Rama to catch the deer*; 104. *Sita*; 105. [no caption].

Lakshmana stands near Rama and Sita, both seated on a low throne. At the centre of the scene Maricha, in the guise of a spotted deer, frolics around. He is depicted twice, to suggest his roaming about. In the following scene Sita is under the guard of Lakshmana, while Rama is away pursuing the deer. In the last scene of this sequence Sita is alone: Lakshmana has gone to look for Rama.

20. Sita's abduction (nos. 106–109)

106. *Sita brings food for Ravana and is abducted*; 107. *Ravana hides away his chariot, comes to ask food from Sita, and once she gave it to him, he abducts her in the chariot*; 108. *He* [Jatayu] *sees that Ravana abducts Sita and wages battle against him*; 109. *Jatayumuni.*

Two episodes are conflated here: Ravana's arrival at the exiles' hut and the actual abduction of Sita. Sita still carrying a ball of rice in her hand and Ravana disguised as an ascetic, with a begging bowl in his hands, are in the chariot. In the next scene Ravana engages a fierce battle with Jatayu, depicted here as a winged ascetic with wild flowing hair. The presence of two birds may suggest that this duel takes place in the sky.

21. Rama chases the golden deer (nos. 110–112)

110. *Rama chases the deer and shoots an arrow*; 111. *Maricha dies and falls down*; 112. *Rama kills Maricha with an arrow. He dies, and falling down, resumes his real form as Maricha*; 113–114. *Rama tells Lakshmana that it is not safe to leave a woman alone in the forest. He asks him to go back to see if she is in the hut.*

22. Rama and Lakshmana meet Jatayu (nos. 115–118)

115–117. When Rama and Lakshmana return to look for Sita, Jatayumuni informs them that she has been abducted by Ravana and that he [Ravana] has cut his wings; 118. The dying Jatayumuni tells them about Sita and passes away.

Kishkindhakanda

23. Rama and Lakshmana arrive in Kishkindha (nos. 119–124)

119. [no caption]; 120. Lakshmana sees the monkey on the tree. While Rama was resting on his lap, it breaks a branch of the tree and throws it down. Lakshmana is angry and shoots an arrow at it because he was waking up Rama, and chases it away; 121–122. [no captions]; 123–124. Sri Rama wakes up [illegible]. Hanuman comes and bows, pays homage to him and asks why he has come. Rama says that Sita was abducted by Ravana, and requests his help to get her back. Hanuman says: "I have other monkeys that can help and will bring them also." He returns bringing the others, and Rama asks Vali [probably this is a slip of the pen for Sugriva] to help him. Vali [Sugriva] promises to do so.

Rama, exhausted, rests his head on Lakshmana's lap. They are beneath the tree on which perches a diminutive monkey, none other but Hanuman, sent by Sugriva to find out who the two brothers are. Lakshmana aims an arrow at the creature, who throws branches on the resting Rama.[14] To Rama's left stand two *vanaras* [monkeys] with hands folded in *anjali mudra*.

24. Rama fells the seven trees and kills Vali (nos. 125–128) (fig. 24)

125. Rama; 126. The arrow he [Rama] shoots pierces the seven trees; 127. Vali. He sits on the other side of the seven trees; 128. Sugriva and Vali are fighting against one another. Rama aims the arrow at Vali; he holds it with his hand. When he (Vali) was about to die he asks Rama to protect his brother.

Fig. 24

Rama aims his arrow at the seven trees. The actual felling of the trees is not shown, but the focus of the scene is Vali, fatally wounded, trying to extract Rama's arrow from his chest. The fight between Vali and Sugriva is not illustrated but just mentioned in the caption. Here again, two distinct incidents are combined into one. According to the Valmikian and other versions of the story, the felling of the seven trees is one of the tests that Rama has to undergo, before Sugriva is persuaded of his valour. The episode of Vali's killing occurs later in the narrative.

Sundarakanda

25. The search for Sita: Hanuman crosses the ocean (nos. 129–134) (fig. 25)

    129. *The monkey-army*; 130. *Lakshmana*; 131. *Rama*; 132. *Rama asks Hanuman to go* [to Lanka] *meet Sita and come back*; 133. *On his way to Sita he must cross the ocean*; 134. *The ocean.*

Fig. 25

26. Hanuman finds Sita in Lanka (nos. 135–139)

    135. *Hanuman finds Sita's whereabouts. He sits on a tree and tells her all the news. Sita sits beneath the tree. Hanuman sits on the tree*; 136. [no caption]; 137. *Sita*; 138. *Trisharei* [Vibhishana's daughter, Trijata]; 139. [no caption].

27. Hanuman wrecks Ravana's garden (nos. 140–144)

    140. *Hanuman, having found Sita, tries to destroy the garden and attacks all the guards that were around. He uproots all the trees and tosses them in the air*; 141–142. *Hanuman uproots the trees, beats Ravana's guards and kills them*; 143. *Indrajit comes to attack Hanuman. His arrows do not hit him; Hanuman stops them. Indrajit is amazed*; 144. *Indrajit.*

28. Hanuman is taken captive by Indrajit (nos. 145–150)

    145–147. [no captions]; 148. *Hanuman says to Indrajit* [illegible]; 149. [no caption]; 150. *Hanuman is taken captive*; 151–152. [no captions].

29. A council scene (nos. 153–156)

    153–154 [no captions]; 155. *Malyavan gives advice to Ravana*; 156. *Indrajit tells his father that it would be better to imprison Sita.*

30. Hanuman in Ravana's presence (nos. 157–159) (fig. 30)

    157. *Ravana tries to hit Hanuman. He raises his hand, but Hanuman* [escapes] *high up*; 158. *Monkey. Hanuman coils his tail and sits high up*; 159. *This is the monkey that destroyed the garden. Ravana commands that its tail should be set on fire.*

Fig. 30

Hanuman, seated on his coiled tail, kicks Ravana's head knocking his crown off. The artist conflated two stories. The first one, the well-known episode in which Hanuman irritates Ravana by sitting at the same level as the king on his coiled tail. The other is that of Vali's son, Angada, who steals Ravana's crown. Rama sends Angada to Ravana on a last-ditch diplomatic mission to avoid a war. The mission fails miserably. Angada, however, manages to kill the guards, to destroy one of the towers in Ravana's palace, steal his crown, and take it back to Rama's camp.

31. Ravana, Kumbhakarna and Malyavan in council (nos. 160–166)

160. Ravana; 161. Kumbhakarna tells Ravana to let Sita go, otherwise they will be in great trouble; 162. Malyavan also tells him [Ravana] to let Sita go otherwise they will be in great trouble; 163. A third person advises Ravana: "When a monkey comes and makes such havoc, it is better to let Sita go." "If you let her go," he advises him, "we can be safe"; 164. [no caption]; 165. Indrajit says, "Please do not get angry, father, I myself will go and fight"; 166. A messenger comes and tells that Rama has arrived with his army.

Yuddhakanda

32. Preparing for the war (nos. 167–174)

167. After meeting Sita, Hanuman returns and crosses the water again to report his adventures to Rama; 168. The ocean; 169. All these are the monkeys who came to help Rama; 170. Sugriva [probably this figure is Vibhishana]; 171. Hanuman tells Rama of his meeting with Sita; 172–173. Lakshmana says to Rama: "We should go to fight against Ravana"; 174. Monkey.

33. Rama and Lakshmana are kidnapped and Hanuman rescues them (nos. 175–183)

175. Vibhishana says to Rama and Lakshmana: "This is Rahu kala time [inauspicious time of the day], *after which we can assemble the troops. Until then Rama and Lakshmana should be well protected." Hanuman places his tail around them forming a big canopy. Rama. Lakshmana; 176–177. Malyavan*[15] *[Mayiliravana], by his magic, makes everybody go to sleep. He then kidnaps Rama and Lakshmana with a view to sacrifice them to Kali;* (fig. 33.1)

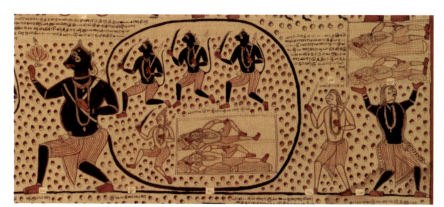

Fig. 33.1

Fig. 33.2

178. Hanuman asks the water-carrier woman: "Hey, woman, where have Rama and Lakshmana been hidden?" She replies that they have been taken to the Kali Temple to be sacrificed; 179. He captures Malyavan [Mayiliravana], *cuts him to pieces and sacrifices him to Kali; 180. The water-carrier has water in her pot; 181. Hanuman discovers the box in which Rama and Lakshmana have been hidden; 182. The Kali Temple.* (fig. 33.2)

Hanuman encircles with his long tail the encampment in which are a group of three monkeys and Vibhishana while Rama and Lakshmana rest lying down in a box.

Mayiliravana is shown twice. Armed with two clubs he approaches Hanuman's tail and the sleeping brothers. The actual kidnapping is not shown, but, when depicted for the second time, Mayiliravana carries on his head the box in which Rama and Lakshmana are fast asleep.

The next scene is packed with action. In the top register, Hanuman brandishes a sword and addresses a woman who carries a pot under her arm. He then grabs Mayiliravana by his hair tuft, with a blow of his sword decapitates him, and cuts his body into pieces. In the lower register, the water carrier appears again, without her pot, she indicates to Hanuman the way to the Kali Temple; the box containing Rama and Lakshmana is placed opposite the image of the goddess. Hanuman enters the temple and rescues them.

34. Hanuman fights against Indrajit (nos. 183–185)

183. Hanuman fights against Indrajit's army; 184. The rakshasa army; 185. Hanuman cuts everybody into pieces. Dead people [in the middle of the scene].

35. Indrajit and the *nagapasha* (serpent-noose) (nos. 186–191)

186. Indrajit; 187. Indrajit fights and aims a volley of arrows towards Lakshmana. Horse; 188. Lakshmana fights against Indrajit; 189. Lakshmana. Horse; 190. Indrajit binds Lakshmana and his followers with the nagapasha; 191. When Rama hears that they had been bound by the nagapasha, he concentrates his mind on Garuda, and thus they are released from the nagapasha.

The serpent-noose is depicted as a large cobra encircling Lakshmana and five *vanaras* among which is Hanuman. This imaginative way of depicting this incident is reminiscent of the scene in which Hanuman's tail draws a magic circle around the princes, prior to their kidnapping by Mayiliravana (no. 33). The spell is broken by the arrival of Garuda.

36. Indrajit's death (nos. 192–198)

192. The monkey army; 193. Lakshmana and his army are fiercely fighting against Indrajit; 194. Indrajit and Lakshmana face each other in combat. Indrajit. 195. Dead Indrajit; 196. These are all the soldiers that followed Indrajit in battle; 197. Hanuman cuts into pieces all Indrajit's followers and scatters their limbs around; 198. Hanuman.

37. Jambavan fights against the *rakshasas* (nos. 199–200)

199. Sambuva [Jambavan]; *200. Sambuva fights the rakshasas and kills them.*

38. Hanuman fights against Kumbhakarna (nos. 201–202)

201. Kumbhakarna. Kumbhakarna and Hanuman fight against each other; 202. Hanuman catches the arrows and bends them. He uproots the trees.

39. Kumbhakarna's death (nos. 203–206)

203. Kumbhakarna; 204. Kumbhakarna is dead; 205. Lakshmana aims arrows at Kumbhakarna and decapitates him; 206. Jambavan and Angada; 207. [no caption], number missing.

In the traditional version of the story Kumbhakarna is decapitated by Rama's arrow and not by Lakshmana's.

40. Battle scenes (nos. 208–210)

208. After having beaten them, Hanuman exterminates the rakshasa army; 209. The rakshasa army; 210. Sugriva attacks the rakshasa army. He beats and kills them.

41. Lakshmana fights against Ravana and is wounded (nos. 211–219)

211. Lakshmana; 212. Lakshmana fights against Ravana. The latter throws his Danda-astra [a magical weapon], *but Lakshmana diverts it with his arrows; 213.* [no caption]; *214. Ravana; 215. Ravana throws his sword, hits Lakshmana in the chest, and he falls down. Hanuman comes running to his help, lifts him and takes him to Rama.*

42. Hanuman brings the *Sanjivi Parvata* (nos. 216–220)

216. Jambavan [no caption]; *217. Vibhishana; 218–219. Rama, with Lakshmana lying on his lap, cries. He calls Jambavan and asks to heal him. Jambavan tells him that there is a mountain called Sanjivi, on which some medicine grows. Rama sends Hanuman to fetch it; 220. This is the medicine mountain. Hanuman has forgotten the name of the medicinal herb, and so brings back the whole mountain.*

This is the first appearance of Rama after the Patala Lanka (no. 33) incident. All along, the action was led by Hanuman and Lakshmana.

43. Rama fights against Ravana (nos. 221–227)

221. Because of the medicine he [Hanuman] *brought, Lakshmana revives and all the monkeys rejoice. They accompany him in the battle against Ravana; 222. Lakshmana; 223. Rama on his chariot. Rama shoots arrows to cut Ravana's heads; 224. Ravana retaliates and shoots a volley of arrows; 225. Ravana on his chariot; 226. The rakshasa army is massacred: Ravana's hands, legs, chest, his ten heads and his crowns all fall.* [This is his] *Body; 227. Dead rakshasas.*

44. The end of the war (nos. 228–230)

228. Sugriva fights against the rakshasa army and kills them; 229. Hanuman kills the enemies with his club. Hanuman; 230. The monkey army.

45. Vibhishana's coronation (nos. 231–234)

231. Vibhishana; 232. Sri Rama calls Vibhishana: now that Ravana has been killed he will become king; 233. He [Rama] *summons Hanuman and asks him to fetch Sita* [in red]. *Hanuman listens to Rama's words respectfully; 234. Lakshmana.*

46. Sita is reunited with Rama, Vibhishana pays homage to Rama (nos. 235–240)

235. Vibhishana is coronated king and rules the country; 236. Trisharei [Trijata] *tells Sita to go, helps her, and lets her go* [not clear]; *237. Angada; 238. Tambi* [Angada's younger brother]; *239. Hanuman comes to escort Sita; 240. Hanuman and Sugriva escort Sita; 241. Trisharei; 242. Sita; 243. Trisharei and Vibhishana pay their respects to Rama and Lakshmana. They say: "We are your slaves", and they leave.*

The emphasis here is on Vibhishana's coronation and on his devotion to Rama, rather than on the dramatic events leading to the reunion of Rama and Sita.

47. Return to Ayodhya (nos. 244–247)

244. Lakshmana; 245. Sita; 246. Having completed their twelve-years' exile, Sita, Rama and Lakshmana commence their walk back home. Rama; 247. Bharata and other kings come to welcome them.

In this retelling there is no hint of Sita's fire ordeal, and of the allies accompanying Rama back to Ayodhya in the aerial chariot. The exiles' return to Ayodhya is unusually low-key.

48. Rama's coronation (nos. 248–259)

248. Hanuman; 249. Rama; 250. Sita. Sita and Rama seated on the throne; 251. Kaikesi (Kaikeyi) and her servant; 252. Fly-whisk bearer; 253. Trumpet player; 254. Lakshmana; 255. Bharata; 256. Simittirai [Sumitra]; 257. Servant; 258. Kuni [Manthara]; 259. [no caption].

Uttarakanda

49. Kusha and Lava fight against Rama's army (nos. 260–265)

260. Sri Rama's army; 261 Rama. Rama arrives in the forest, Kusha and Lava wound him with their arrows; 262. Being wounded by the arrows, Rama faints; 263. Sita comes and revives Rama; 264. Lava; 265. Kusha.

50. The story of Sita and Valmiki (nos. 266–269)

266. Sita talks to Valmiki saying that... [illegible]; 267. Valmiki; 268. Lava and Kusha; 269. Sita puts them in the cradle. Cradle.

This section of the narrative is a flashback. It deals, probably, with the birth of Sita's twins in Valmiki's hermitage. Sita, carrying a water pot under her arm, talks to the sage Valmiki; in the foreground Lava and Kusha sit under the watchful gaze of the sage. Nearby is a large cradle, in which the two infants lie sucking their thumbs.

51. The reunion of Rama with Sita and his sons (nos. 270–275)

270. Valmiki; 271. Trumpet player; 272. Sita; 273. The two sons pay their respects to Rama. [He says] "Without knowing I was fighting against my boys". He takes the boys with him; 274. Tarai [trumpet] player; 275. Chinna mayuru [trumpet] player.

52. End of the story (nos. 276–279)

276. [no caption]; 277. Sita; 278. Rama, Sita and their sons on the throne. 279. [no caption].

Notes

1. The meeting of Lakshmana and the *rakshasi* Ayomukhi is found in both Valmiki's *Ramayana* (*Aranyakanda* 69th *sarga*) and Kamban *Iramavataram* (3-9-1-101).

2. This episode has not been illustrated in the *kalamkaris* from Andhra and Tamil Nadu under review here.

3. This is probably a local variation of the name Mayiliravana. Malyavan was the elder brother of Ravana's maternal grandfather. He was the chief counsellor of Ravana. He was against the war with Rama and tried to convince Ravana to let Sita go. In order to avoid confusion, I used the name Mayiliravana.

4. For a very similar background, see S. Cohen 2006: 56–80, in particular fig. 9 on p. 65.

5. 1) black with rust red hands and feet—often used for some deities, e.g. Vinayaka, the *vanaras*, and occasionally the *rakshasas*.

    2) light brown with rust red hands and feet—used generally for Rama, Sita, Vibhishana, etc.

    3) light brown, black body, red hands and feet—Kumbhakarna.

    4) rust red—ascetics, various deities, ancillary figures, Lakshmana, Ravana, etc.

6. Surya's face is surrounded by twelve rays symbolizing the twelve Adityas.

7. Garuda's feet crush two large cobras. This detail derives from classic iconography where Garuda wears cobras as anklets.

8. The inspiration for this rendering of Hanuman derives from the icon of Vira Anjaneya: Hanuman running with raised right arm ready to hit an enemy, and carrying an uprooted tree in his left. Here the uprooted tree has become a lotus.

9. As already mentioned (see p. 80), in this work Kuni, usually associated with Kaikeyi, is Queen Sumitra's servant.

10. Although Kuni is depicted plotting with Sumitra against Rama, it is finally Kaikeyi who sends Rama into exile. This conforms to the traditional version of the narrative.

11. According to the tradition, however, the exiles pay homage, first of all to Kausalya, the elder queen and Rama's mother, and then to Kaikeyi. In this version of the narrative Kausalya is not mentioned.

12. At this point in time, according to other traditions, Bharata and Shatrughna are not in Ayodhya but visiting a relative.

13. The caption mentions twelve years of exile, whereas in general the number of years is given as fourteen.

14. The Malay version of the story, *Hikayat Seri Rama,* narrates how Hanuman perches on a tree, and throws broken twigs at the sleeping Rama in order to attract his attention. This incident is part of an involved story, according to which Rama turns out to be Hanuman's father (Stutterheim [1925] 1989: 39).

15. See n. 3.

Ramayana, selected scenes (cat. 6–8)

The following three *kalamkaris* from the Madurai area illustrate specific parts of the *Ramayana*: the *Balakanda*; the final battle between Rama and Ravana from the *Yuddhakanda*; and the *Ramapattabhisheka,* Rama's coronation. It is probable that these three hangings might have been part of a set depicting the complete story of Rama.

Balakanda MADURAI

The narratives of the *Balakanda* and the *Yuddhakanda* are laid out on four registers and dispense with a central scene. The central tableau, flanked on either side by four vignettes, depicts the *Ramapattabhisheka*. In all three cloths the registers are divided by a narrow band enlivened by red dots; white rosettes appear on the panels' red background. The scenes flow one into the other without solution of continuity, and bear brief explanatory captions in Tamil.

The narrative commences with Kalaikottu—i.e. Rishyashringa—travelling to Ayodhya to perform *putrakameshti yaga*, a ritual which will ensure that King Dasharatha will have a son. The story follows the usual line. An interesting feature of this work is the depiction of Rama shooting arrows at Kaikeyi's [Kaikesi] hunchback servant, called here Kuni, i.e. 'hunchback' (fig. 10). This rarely illustrated episode, highlighted in Kamban's *Iramavataram*, explains her animosity against Rama, and, eventually, her role in persuading Kaikesi to banish him. The artist, conscious of its importance, has given it the prominence it deserves.

The episodes of the killing of Tataka and of Vishvamitra's sacrifice are shown in reverse chronological order.

The names of the two sages, Vasishtha and Vishvamitra, are confused in the captions. The latter appears on the scene only when Rama and Lakshmana are adolescents, whereas Vasishtha, as royal chaplain and counsellor of Dasharatha,

6. Balakanda
IM 24-1911
Dimensions: 195 x 270.5 cm
Date: 19th century
Provenance: Madurai region
Captions: in Tamil

plays a pivotal role before the birth of the princes, during their education and their training in the martial arts. This confusion between two sages is not unknown and it has been noted in other renderings of the *Ramayana*.[1]

On the back of the cloth (fig. 20) are some preparatory drawings, which reveal the technical mastery of the artist and give an insight into what is one of the early phases in the intricate process of *kalamkari* preparation. Characteristic of this work are depictions of European-style chairs and hats, as well as the lavish use of green pigment.

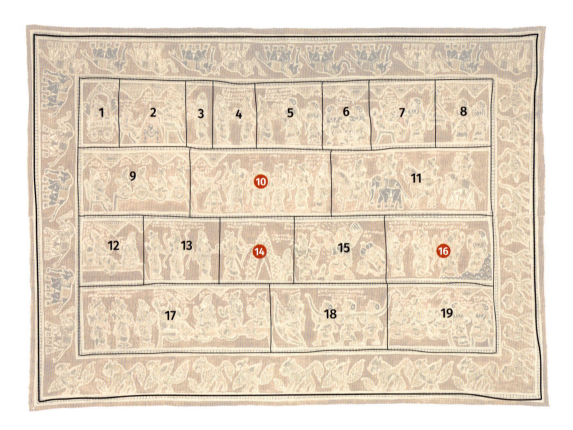

CAPTIONS

Top register

1. *Kalaikottu* [Rishyashringa] *maharishi* [on his way to Ayodhya].
   There is no horse to draw the conveyance.

2. *Kalaikottu maharishi performs the yaga. The bhuta* [spirit] *appears.*

3. *Kalaikottu maharishi gives the ball of rice to Vishvamitra* [Vasishtha].

4. *Vishvamitra* [Vasishtha] *gives the pindas to Dasharatha raja.*

5. *Dasharatha raja gives the pindas to Kausalya, Kaikesi and Sumitra; Sumitra.*

6. *It was the time for the baby to be born of Kaikesi; midwife* [?].

   A midwife sits on a low stool between Kaikesi, who is in the process of giving birth to Bharata, and an attendant supports her. The artist introduces Kaikesi here, rather than along with the other two queens, thus making the viewer aware of her pivotal role in the development of the narrative.

7. *Kausalya is giving the baby to Dasharatha maharaja.*

8. *Sumitra is rocking the cradle.*

Second register

9. *Vishvamitra* [Vasishtha] *teaching; Ramasvami, Lakshmana, Bharata, Shatrughna.*

10. [From right to left] *Vishvamitra* [Vasishtha] *teaches them archery; Lakshmana, Bharata, Shatrughna; Ramasvami aims the arrow at Kuni.* (fig. 10)

    This episode has to be read from right to left: Vasishtha, with the hand raised in teaching attitude, looks on as his charges practise archery. Rama, the first from left, is depicted shooting an arrow at Kuni who is on the verge of entering the palace. Kuni is bent into two by age, walks with a stick, her distended breasts sag from her emaciated ribs, and her toothless mouth, open in a scream, are dramatically rendered. Being hit by Rama's missile, she turns back toward the prince, reprimanding him sharply.

Fig. 10

11. *Ramasvami on the elephant, Lakshmana on the horse. Bharata, Shatrughna.*

    Contrary to the caption, Rama and Bharata ride horses; Lakshmana and Shatrughna, elephants.

Third register

12. *Vishvamitra and Dasharatha maharaja [talking] together.*

13. *Vishvamitra is taking the children to safeguard his yaga.*

14. *Lakshmana arrives at the yagashala. Vishvamitra lights the fire in the yagashala.* (fig. 14)

Fig. 14   *Drawing on the Reverse, see p. 102*

As already mentioned, the place in the narrative sequence and the visual treatment of this episode are unusual. Subahu and Maricha, the *rakshasas* who pollute the sacrificial flame, do not appear; furthermore, the artist has shown Lakshmana as the sole protector of the *yaga*. With his arrows he builds a canopy above the sacrificial flame. Vishvamitra sits near it, pouring *ghee* into the flame.

15. *Ramasvami kills Tataka; Tataka is dead.*

16. *While Vishvamitra talks to Ramasvami and Lakshmana, Ahalya's curse is removed.* (fig. 16)

Fig. 16

This is one of the pivotal incidents of the *Balakanda*, and, instead of creating a devotional tableau, the artist renders it with refreshing informality.

The sage, with raised arm, talks to Rama, who while walking, turns around towards him and Lakshmana, to reply. At that very moment his foot brushes against a pile of rocks, from which emerges Ahalya, with her hands in *anjali mudra*. Rama, however, steeped in his conversation with Vishvamitra, seems fully unaware of her presence.

Fourth register

17. *Ramasvami, Lakshmana and Vishvamitra, all walk together; Sanaku* (Janaka) *maharaja's house; Vishvamitra asks for his daughter* [to be married to Rama]; *Vishvamitra, Rama, Lakshmana.*

18. *Ramasvami; they bring the bow and Ramasvami breaks it.*

    The narrative sequence here proceeds from right to left: three servants of Janaka carry the huge bow of Shiva. Without effort Rama lifts the mighty bow and while stringing it, breaks it.

19. *Vishvamitra sends a message to Ayodhya; the minister writes the letter; Sanaku maharaja; Sita-Lakshmi gives some pearls to her companion.*

    The writer of the captions, by calling Sita as Sita-Lakshmi, stresses the fact that as Rama is an aspect of Vishnu, Sita is an aspect of Lakshmi.

Borders

The top and the left border display a procession of elephants; the right border, lions; the bottom border, fabulous *yali* [leogryph]-like creatures with foliated tails and paws, and *hamsas* [geese] with exuberant feathers.

Reverse

An unusual feature of this *kalamkari* is that at the back of it there is a register-and-a-half of drawings (fig. 20) behind the fourth and third register of the painted version. They are remarkable for the assuredness and clarity of the line: there are no hesitations and no corrections.

The incomplete series of drawings commences from the conversation of Vishvamitra and Dasharatha, and ends with the sequence of scenes leading to Shiva's bow being broken by Rama. If the project had been completed, the whole sequence of events, beginning from Kalaikottu *maharishi*'s arrival in Ayodhya until the schooling of the princes, would have been omitted, but the scenes of the four marriages, of the Ikshvaku princes with the Mithila princesses, would probably have been included in the last two rows.

The painted version ends just before the wedding celebrations, which is very unusual. It is possible that another *kalamkari*, devoted uniquely to the festivities and rituals connected to the royal weddings and the return of the brides and grooms to Ayodhya, had been planned, but there is no way of ascertaining this.

Fig. 20

First register (behind the fourth register of the painted version)

1. Conversation of King Dasharatha with Vishvamitra *maharishi*.

2. The sage and his charges on their way to the forest. Vishvamitra carries in his hands not only a chaplet, but also a bell (?). In the painted version, his right hand is empty.

3. Lakshmana builds the arrow canopy above the *yagashala* while Vishvamitra feeds the flame, pouring in it *ghee* (see fig. 14).

4. Rama's encounter with Tataka: a slight variant from the painted version is that only her beheaded body and head lie in the foreground, and not a severed arm.

5. Ahalya's emancipation.

Second register (behind the third register of the painted version)

6. A conversation between Janaka and Vishvamitra in the presence of the princes. The painted version depicts Vishvamitra, Rama and Lakshmana walking towards Mithila.

7. In the episode of the breaking of the bow, a fourth figure appears following the three servants, carrying Shiva's weapon.

The series of drawings ends at this point.

Note

1. British Museum, Asia As1966,01.496, see p. 69.

Yuddhakanda MADURAI

The *Yuddhakanda* offers an ample repertoire of themes. Although there is no general consensus regarding the episodes that should be illustrated, the most popular are: the building of the bridge to Lanka; Rama and Lakshmana succumbing to Indrajit's *nagapasha,* serpent-noose; the awakening of Kumbhakarna; and the decisive battle between Rama and Ravana.

This hanging focuses on the latter episode. The composition is laid out in four rows in which various phases of the action are illustrated in detail: from the arrival of Ravana on the battlefield, to his death. Formally this work is very similar to the one illustrating the battle between Karna and Arjuna in cat. 11. The Rama–Ravana *yuddha* (battle) hanging is more exciting because of the presence of the monkeys, especially Hanuman, who appears in many different roles and is, undoubtedly, the main character of the

7. Yuddhakanda
IM 25-1911
Dimensions: 193 x 277 cm
Date: 19th century
Provenance: Madurai region
Captions: in Tamil

painted narrative. He is ubiquitous, ever alert and ever ready to assist Rama in his mission: he carries Rama on his shoulders; armed with an uprooted tree and the occasional boulder, he fights against a posse of *rakshasas*; then, again, against Ravana and destroys his chariot not only once, but at least twice. In this work, Rama and a number of his allies consistently wear *kulayis* (tall caps) rather than the more usual crowns or headbands.

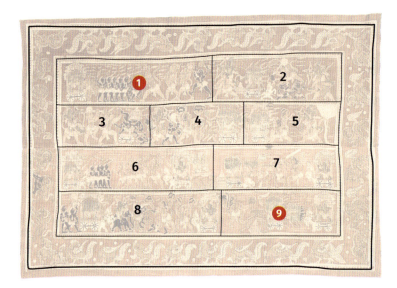

CAPTIONS

Top register

1. *Ravana goes to battle with his rakshasa army; Avakunda; Sugriva; Kumrusuna fight; Ramasvami fights against Ravana.* (fig. 1)

Fig. 1

Preceded by seven *rakshasas*, all armed with different types of clubs, Ravana drives towards the battlefield on a horse-drawn chariot. He shoots volleys of arrows against Avakunda, Sugriva and Rama's other allies. He has nine heads (see cat. 15, n.4), twelve right- and eleven left-arms. All but the lower pair, in which he carries bow-and-arrow, are devoid of attributes. All the *vanaras* are grinning fiercely, showing their sharp, side fangs.

Rama, crowned and bejewelled, rides on Hanuman's shoulders shooting arrows at Ravana. Volleys of arrows enliven the background.

2. *Hanuman attacks Ravana with a tree; Ramasvami shoots arrows at Ravana.*

Second register

3. *Ramasvami* [attacks Ravana] *with the kodanda* [bow]; *Avakunda attacks one of the rakshasas...* [unclear]

4. [Unfortunately the captions are very faint and difficult to decipher.]

   Rama stands on the hands of a *vanara* and aims his arrows at Ravana. In the meantime, Hanuman, armed with piles of boulders, unmindful of a *rakshasa* who pursues him armed with an uprooted tree, attacks Ravana. One of his boulders hits Ravana's chariot. Ravana, however, continues his fight unperturbed. The conveyance's roof, spiked with arrows, falls to the ground among his numerous heads, limbs, and crowns. Despite being severed, Ravana's limbs regenerate and the fight continues. Boulders and volley of arrows fly in the background.

5. The third scene is practically a repetition of the last scene in the first register. Ravana, riding his chariot, is attacked by Hanuman; Rama, whose feet are supported by the hands of a *vanara*, aims his arrows at his foe, while the chariot's roof is hit by one of Hanuman's boulders. A tree concludes the scene.

Third register

6. *The monkey army and the rakshasa army fight against each other; Ramasvami and his army send their arrows.*

   Rama is shown on a chariot for first time—until this point he was carried on the shoulders by a *vanara*—is preceded by four fierce-looking monkeys, and by Hanuman. The latter prepares for a fight. In the background, volleys of arrows shot by Rama land on the *rakshasa* army.

7. [Illegible]... *During the battle, Ramasvami beheads Ravana and throws his heads away; Hanuman beats with a stick* [?]; *Ramasvami shoots his arrows and decapitates Ravana.*

   Rama sits in a chariot, drawn by a winged horse. This is probably an allusion to the divine conveyance sent by Indra.

Fourth register

8. *Ravana goes off to fight; battlefield; Hanuman fights.*

9. *Hanuman uproots hillocks and throws them;* [Ramasvami's] *arrows wound Ravana's throat; he falls and dies; Ramasvami fighting.* (fig. 9)

Fig. 9

The final battle: to the extreme left is Hanuman, armed with boulders, facing Ravana; to the extreme right, Rama, on his chariot, aims his arrows at Ravana who, at the centre, tries desperately to fight off both his adversaries. His chariot is in pieces, his limbs scattered all over the battlefield, he does not give up until Rama's arrows hit him in the throat, killing him. While falling, his hair-knots come loose.

Borders

[Top and bottom] Pecking *hamsas*; small rosettes enliven the background. On the right and left border: lion-like animals. On the lower left corner is a horse, and on the left border, a lion devours an elephant.

Ramapattabhisheka MADURAI

Rama's coronation, the central tableau, follows the traditional iconography as seen in the murals, paintings on paper and on other supports. The main actors of the scene are arranged in different groups: at the top are the royal couple, Rama's brothers, and Vasishtha bearing Rama's crown. Immediately beneath them are the *rishis* present at the function, and a group of ladies, probably the wives of Rama's brothers; Rama's allies, neatly arranged in two rows, come next. Among them are Vibhishana and his followers. Hanuman kneeling before the throne, gently supporting Rama's right foot, has the pride of place. Immediately below him is Sugriva dipping his hand in a large trunk filled with jewels and gifts to be distributed among Rama's allies.

On either side of the central tableau are four vignettes depicting the guests present at the coronation: the seven *rishis*, the rulers of the fifty-six countries,[1] the most distinguished kings, and the representatives of the various communities. The background is adorned by white rosettes.

8. Ramapattabhisheka
IM 26-1911
Dimensions: 193 x 274 cm
Date: 19th century
Provenance: Madurai region
Captions: in Tamil

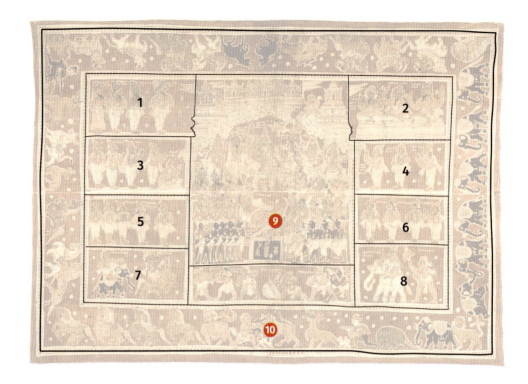

Labels:

Top register [left and right] *Saptarishis* (seven sages)

1. *Valmika, Pannu maharishi, Vishvamitra, Satananda rishi.*
2. *Tandu maharishi, Patanjali maharishi, Kandurupa* [?] *rishi.*

Second register [left]

3. *Rajarajakal* ['king of kings'], *Vedavyasa* [the reputed author of the Mahabharata].
4. *Nara chakravarti* ['universal king'], *and two Gajapatikal.*[2]

Third register [left and right]

5. *The kings of the fifty-six countries.*
6. *The kings of the fifty-six countries.*

Fourth register [left and right]

7. *Devendra; Kubera.*

   Devendra sits on the elephant and is preceded by Kubera riding on a prancing horse.

8. *The representative of the Shudra nations; umbrella bearer.*

Central tableau (fig. 9)

9. Top, beneath the arch: [illegible]... *Lakshmana, Vasishthasvami puts the crown, Ramasvami's crowning ceremony, Sitai Amman, Bharata, Shatrughna.*

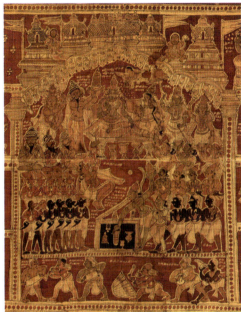

Fig. 9

In a hall capped by a barrel-vaulted roof with seven *kalashas* (finials), flanked by *stupikas* (domes) and squatting lions, Vasishtha *maharishi* officiates at Rama's coronation. Beneath a lobed arch decorated with lotus garlands, Rama and Sita, sumptuously dressed and bejewelled, sit on a throne, with their shoulders leaning against a large bolster. Rama's left leg rests on the seat, while his right foot is reverently supported by Hanuman. To Rama's right are Vasishtha, with the crown in his hands and Lakshmana carrying a fly-whisk. To Sita's left are Bharata and Shatrughna, holding an umbrella and a fly-whisk respectively. To the right of the divine couple sit three *rishis*, and opposite them, to the left, three ladies stand with trays filled with gifts.

Centre: *Hanuman; monkey army; bear army; Sugriva opens the jewel box and gives clothes and jewellery.*

Behind Vibhishana: *ministers.*

Behind Hanuman are five *vanaras* and six bears, with their hands folded in *anjali mudra*. The *vanaras* wear *kulayis*, the bears are bare-headed except for Jambavan. Opposite them are four men, all wearing *kulayis*, with sword and buckler hanging from their belts. In the front row, opposite Jambavan, is Vibhishana, recognisable by his side fangs, accompanied by three of his *rakshasa* ministers. At the centre of the hall is a large box with jewellery items, from which Sugriva picks out a crown and a set of necklaces.

Bottom: *Tavul* [drum] *player, nagasvaram* [wind instrument] *player, tavul player, nagara* [kettle drum] *player, daf* [tambourine] *player, conch blower.*

Borders (fig. 10)

The upper border displays a number of fighting scenes: caparisoned bulls, stags fighting, horsemen duelling.

On the lower border are galloping horses, hunting and martial scenes.

A procession of caparisoned elephants and *yali* adorns the right border, and on the left border are: galloping horses, a hare (?), a bull and an Englishman shooting a deer (or antelope). The background is enlivened by the occasional white rosette.

Top

Left

Right

Bottom

Fig. 10: Borders

Notes

1. See cat. 1, n. 12.
2. The mention of the Nara *chakravarti* and the kings of the Gajapati kingdom among the personalities attending Rama's coronation is very interesting. The Vijayanagara king was known as Narapati, 'king of men'; and the ruler of Odisha and Coastal Andhra was referred to as Gajapati, 'lord of elephants'. There was a third important king, the Ashvapati, 'king of horses', identified with the Mughal emperor, occasionally with the Delhi Sultan. The scribe is aware, albeit vaguely, of the existence of these three powerful dynasties that were pivotal in the history of peninsular India in the pre-modern period. He seems, however, to have forgotten the name of one of them, the Ashvapati, and hence writes: 'two Gajapatikal'.

Krishnacharita COASTAL ANDHRA

The narrative, based largely on that of the tenth book of the *Bhagavata Purana*, is laid out in four concentric bands around the central medallion. It begins with the image of Vatapatrashayi, floating on a banyan leaf on the Primeval Ocean. This is followed by a depiction of the gods and the *dikpalas* asking the deity's help to rid the earth of the tyrant of Mathura, Kamsa. Krishna's childhood and adolescence among the *gopas*, his contests with the demons sent by Kamsa, with Brahma, Indra and Kaliya are shown in detail. The artist and the patron were more interested in the playful and heroic facets of the story. Krishna's dalliance with the *gopis* plays a secondary role.

After the death of Kamsa, Krishna, supported by Balarama, is confronted with the duties of a ruler. He faces Kamsa's father-in-law, Jarasandha, and immediately afterwards, King Kalayavana (fig. 70). The story of Kalayavana, defeated by Krishna's cunning, appears here along with the other rarely depicted incident of the *syamantaka* gem (fig. 75). These incidents are illustrated on the two long panels flanking the central medallion. The recovery of the gem leads to Krishna's contest with Jambavan, the legendary king of the bears and ally of Rama, and eventually to Krishna's marriage with Jambavati. His marriages with Rukmini (no. 73) and with Satyabhama are briefly touched upon.

Surrounded by lotus petals the central tableau shows Krishna enthroned. He sits holding his wives Rukmini and Satyabhama on his thighs, and is surrounded by his other six wives. Beneath the central rosette are two popular incidents: the Churning of the Milk Ocean (no. 83) and the story of Vishnu rescuing the king of the elephants, Gajendra, from the jaws of a crocodile (no. 80).

This canopy, probably made in northern Coastal Andhra, is particularly interesting as it shows a variety of stylistic influences. When Krishna appears as Vishnu, the artist shows him frontally with an oversized head and short arms in a manner reminiscent of the image of Jagannatha at Puri in neighbouring Odisha (e.g. no. 13). The rendering of Krishna's flute is typically Odishan. Its role in the narrative is particularly intriguing: Krishna not only plays the flute to charm mankind and animals, but also uses it as a weapon to kill his adversaries (e.g. no. 56). Krishna's flute and, incidentally, Balarama's ploughshare are perceived not as mere attributes, but as parts or emanations of the respective deity.

Krishnacharita Coastal Andhra

The intricate crowns, the flowering bowers (no. 54), the depiction of the lion (no. 76), and last but not least the appearance of the composite mythical creature, the *navagunjara*, in a medallion (no. 6), all indicate a familiarity with Odishan iconography and motifs. The depiction of Krishna slaying the elephant demon (no. 61) is borrowed from the renderings in sculpture and painting of the story of Madivelaia,[1] a Virashaiva saint popular in Andhra. The depiction of Damodara Krishna follows the 19th-century South Indian iconography. Finally, a number of incidents, especially some of Krishna's pranks (nos. 30–32), are inspired by the songs and poems popular in the Telugu oral tradition.

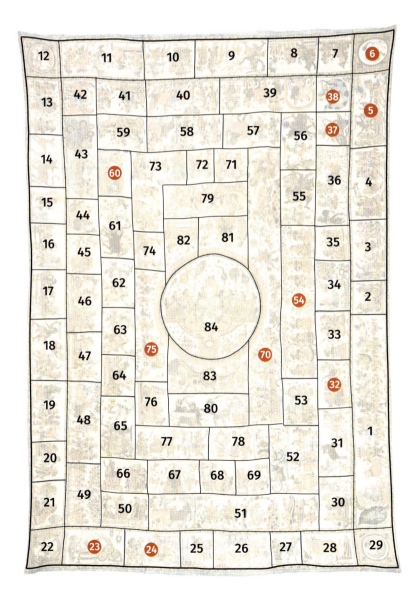

9. Krishnacharita, 'The Story of Krishna'
5447 (IS)
Dimensions: 356 x 258 cm
Date: late 18th or early 19th century
Provenance: Northern Coastal Andhra
Captions: in Telugu

CAPTIONS

1. *All the devatas come to Srimad Narayana asking to protect them. He promises to do so.*
   Labels: *Devendra; Agni; Yamadharma; Nirruti; Varuna; Vayu; Ishana.*

   Vatapatrashayi, sucking his right toe, reclines on a banyan leaf floating on the Primeval Ocean. Unusually, he is shown here with four arms. Vishnu and Lakshmi sit on the nine-headed serpent, Shesha. Opposite the divine couple are, the Earth, in the form of a cow, followed by the four-headed Brahma and the *dikpala*s, a feature noted also in cat. 1 and cat. 2.

2. *Ugrasena and Surasena talking.*

   Surasena, the founder of the Yadava dynasty, converses with Ugrasena, Kamsa's father, former king of Mathura, deposed by his son.

3. *Kamsa; Brahmin; Devaki and Vasudeva celebrating their wedding; Brahmin; Sumangali.*

4. *Band playing; band playing; shenai player.*

   On the left are two trumpet players, unusually attired in long kilts, heavy jackets, a scarf draped on their chests, hats, and one of them, in boots. Possibly this costume is inspired by the uniform of a Scottish regiment.

5. *Vasudeva; Kamsa grabbing Devaki by the hair; Akashvani.* (fig. 5)

   While Kamsa is driving the newly-weds, a voice from the sky, *akashvani*, warns him that their eighth son would kill him. Kamsa, sword in hand, grabs Devaki by the hair and is about to kill her, when Vasudeva promises that they would hand all their sons over to him.

Fig. 5

Fig. 6

6. *Navagunjara* (fig. 6)

   A fabulous winged beast, which has the head of a cock, the hand of a woman carrying a spear,[2] one elephant's leg, one paw of a lion, and one hoof of a cow. It has the body of a humped cow and the tail of a snake. On its body are *chakra* and *shankha*.

7. *He [Kamsa] handcuffs them [Vasudeva and Devaki] and throws them into prison.*

8. *Narada and Kamsa talking. Devaki's children honour... [illegible]*

   The first six sons of Vasudeva and Devaki are surrendered by their parents.

9. *Kamsa kills the children.*
   Labels: *Vasudeva; Devaki.*

   Kamsa proceeds to kill the six children before the eyes of Vasudeva and Devaki.

10. *Sri Krishnasvami speaks to Mayadevi.*

    The goddess Mayadevi, who will descend to earth as the daughter of Yashoda, pays homage to the four-armed Krishna-Vishnu. He is shown frontally with an oversized head and short arms, in a manner reminiscent of the image of Jagannatha at Puri.

11. *While Devaki and Vasudeva rested, Shiva, Brahma, Devendra [Indra] came and talked to them.*
    Label: *Devendra.*

12. *Acrobats inscribed in a circle.*[3]

13. *Vasudeva; Sri Krishna; Devaki.*

    Immediately after his birth Krishna manifests himself in his supreme form to his parents.

14. *This is Kamsa's dog; tiger.*

    The dogs watching the dungeon in which Vasudeva and Devaki are held captive, fell asleep when Krishna was born, thus enabling Vasudeva to carry him to Nanda's settlement. The tiger, as alter ego of Devi, escorts him in his daring expedition across the Yamuna.

15. *Vasudeva takes Krishna where the shepherds live. The Yamuna comes and helps [him].*

    Although not mentioned in the caption, Shesha shelters Vasudeva and baby Krishna under his extended hoods.

16. *While Yashodadevi was asleep, Vasudeva leaves Krishna and takes with him Mayadevi.*

17. *While Kamsa is asleep a rakshasa comes and calls him.*

18. *[In the sky] This is Mayadevi; Kamsa; Devakidevi; Vasudeva.*

    Kamsa brandishes a large sword and is on the verge of killing Yashoda's child, the goddess incarnate. He has grabbed her by the feet, while Devaki holds her arms. At the centre of the scene, the three-headed (?) and six-armed Mayadevi floats on a cloud in the sky.

19. *He [Kamsa] calls Putaki [Putana] and tells her to kill Sri Krishnasvami.*

20. *She [Putaki] is bathing Sri Krishnasvami.*

21. *Putaki takes Krishnasvami in order to kill him.*

    Putaki nurses Krishna who sucks her life away.

22. Acrobats forming a circle with their bodies.

23. *Sri Krishna Bhagavan kills Shakatasura.* (fig. 23)
    Label: *Gopika.*

    Krishna lies in a cradle while a *gopi* rocks him to sleep. He holds onto a rope hanging from the ceiling and half-reclining he kicks the life out of the cart-demon. Shakatasura, a black creature with large round eyes and protruding fangs, emerges from beneath the cart.

Fig. 23   Fig. 24

24. *Sri Krishnasvami kills Trinavarta.* (fig. 24)

    Trinavarta, under the form of a whirlwind, armed with a *trishula*, snatches Krishna away into the sky. The infant, however, becomes 'heavy as a mountain', grips the demon around his throat and kills him. On the left: Krishna comforts Yashoda.

25. *The gopika churns the buttermilk and Sri Krishnasvami comes to take it.*

26. *Sri Krishnasvami taking butter; gopas; [illegible]; Sri Krishnasvami.*

    Accompanied by two companions Krishna stands on a pedestal and reaches for four large pots hanging from a pole fixed to the ceiling. On the extreme right, Krishna stands on the back of an old woman, bent into two and leaning on a stick, who berates the boys for their unruly behaviour.

27. *Sri Krishna milks the cow and gives [the milk] to Yashoda.*

28. *Sri Krishna milks the cow.*

29. Acrobats forming a circle with their bodies.

30. *While the shepherd and his wife were sleeping Sri Krishnasvami [comes and] scares them with a snake.*

This and the following two episodes drawn from the local tradition have been incorporated into the classic repertoire of Krishna's pranks.

31. *Sri Krishnasvami ties the hair of his friends together.*

    On the left, Krishna is shown running after a startled cow to whose tail the pigtail of a *gopa* has been tied. Krishna claps his hands and the unfortunate boy is dragged away by the frightened animal. To the right, Krishna looks at two *gopas*, whose pigtails he has tied together.

32. *While the shepherd and his wife were sleeping, Sri Krishnasvami* [comes and] *scares them with a scorpion.* (fig. 32)

33. *The milkmaids complain to Yashoda about* [the behaviour] *of Sri Krishnasvami.*

34. *Sri Krishnasvami is tied to the mortar. Narada.*

    Krishna is tied to a mortar wedged between two trees. He crawls on all fours pulling the rope which ties him to the mortar, and the two trees are uprooted. Two *gandharvas*, with their hands folded in *anjali mudra*, emerge among the branches and foliage. The sage Narada looks on from a cloud in the sky.

Fig. 32

35. *The gopika tells Yashoda that Krishna has been eating mud. She asks him to open his mouth.*

36. *Nakshasura is killed. The cows are grazing.*

37. *Sri Krishnasvami kills Bakasura.* (fig. 37)

    Krishna tears Baka's beak apart with his hands while he firmly steps on it with his left foot. The *asura*'s huge body falls out of the heron's mouth.

38. *Sri Krishnasvami kills Aghasura.* (fig. 38)

    Krishna steps on the coiled body of Aghasura, forcibly opening its mouth with his left hand and his feet. In the right hand he brandishes his flute.

Fig. 37   Fig. 38

39. *Brahma conceals all the boys. Sri Krishnasvami manifests himself to him* [i.e. Brahma] *in his divine form* [see no. 10].
    Labels: *Cowherds and cows; Brahma; Cowherds and cows.*

40. *Balarama; Cowherds grazing the cows.*

41. *A gopika and Krishna making love; Sri Krishnasvami dallying with a gopika.*

42. *Cowherds and cows.*

43. *Kalinga. Sri Krishnasvami offers salvation to the wives of Kalinga.*

    On the left, Krishna, entangled in the coils of Kalinga, fights with him in the River Yamuna. At the centre he dances on the nine hoods of the snake, holding his tail in his right hand. Two of Kalinga's wives surface from the depths pleading Krishna to spare the life of their husband.

44. *Yashoda; Balarama and gopikas.*

45. *Sri Krishnasvami devours the fire.*

46. **Labels:** *Sri Krishnasvami; Balarama; Nanda; Yashoda.*

47. *The Brahmins were reading. A cowherd comes and tells them* [that he is hungry, but he is turned away].
    Label: *Cowherd.*

48. *Balarama and Sri Krishnasvami give salvation to the Brahmin girls.*

    While the Brahmins refuse to give food to the cowherds, their wives come to feed them.[4]

49. **Label:** *Ponna tree.* [Krishna steals the clothes of the *gopikas*.]

50. **Labels:** *Balarama; Sri Krishnasvami; Nanda talking; Yashoda.*

51. **Labels:** *Cows; shepherds; shepherds carrying a yoke; Sri Krishnasvami.*

    Nanda performing a yaga; Balarama.

52. *Balarama; Sri Krishnasvami lifting the Govardhana hill; Nanda; Yashoda.*

    In the sky, Varuna sits on his *makara* and holds a noose (?). Opposite him, Indra on Airavata brandishes the *vajra*.

53. *Devendra and Varuna worship Sri Krishnasvami.*

    Varuna and Indra pay homage to Krishna. He is shown frontally, and carries the Vaishnava attributes in his upper hands.

54. *Sri Krishnasvami plays flute to the gopikas.* (fig. 54)

Fig. 54

55. *A rakshasa abducts the gopikas. Sri Krishnasvami kills him.*

56. Labels: *Balarama; Sri Krishnasvami; Gatakasura.*

Krishna brandishes the flute like a club, and with his left hand punches the donkey (?) between his eyes, while kicking it. The *asura* still brandishing sword and shield emerges from the donkey's carcass. Balarama looks on.

57. *Balarama. Sri Krishnasvami kills Vrishabhasura.*

Krishna, holding his flute in the right hand, sticks his left hand deep into the bull's throat, while kicking the animal to death. The *asura* armed with *trishula* and shield emerges from the bull's carcass.

58. Labels: *Balarama; Sri Krishnasvami; Akrura; cows; Akrura.*

59. *Akrura is driving the chariot.*
Labels: *Balarama; Sri Krishnasvami.*

Kamsa sends Akrura to fetch Krishna and Balarama to Mathura for the great tournament, with a view to killing them. On seeing him, the brothers immediately divine the plot behind this invitation.

60. *While Akrura was bathing, Sri Krishnasvami manifests himself* [to Akrura] *in his real form.* (fig. 60)

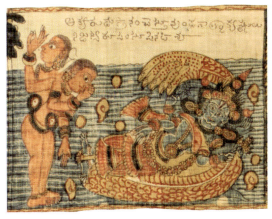
Fig. 60

On the way to Mathura, Akrura stops to take his bath in the Yamuna. As soon as he plunges under the water he sees Krishna and Balarama. He emerges from the water looking for them: they sit on the chariot. He plunges again into the water and sees Vishnu reclining on the coils of the five-hooded Shesha. Returning to the surface Akrura turns around towards the foregoing scene (no. 59), to ascertain that Krishna and Balarama were where he had left them.

61. Labels: *Balarama; Gajasuramardana* [i.e. Krishna as killer of the elephant demon]; *Sri Krishnasvami.*

Krishna grabs with his right hand the trunk of the elephant, while brandishing the flute as if it were a club, in his left. His right foot is firmly planted on the ground, and with the left he kicks the life out of the animal.

62. *Balarama kills Mushtika.*

Balarama, brandishing his ploughshare, fights against Kamsa's prize-fighter, Mushtika.

63. *Sri Krishnasvami kills Chanura.*

The layout of this scene is similar to that of no. 62. Krishna, using his flute as a weapon, parries the attacks of Kamsa's second prize-fighter, Chanura.

64. *Sri Krishnasvami kills Kamsa.*

Kamsa reclines on a bed, when Krishna surprises him in his sleep and pierces his throat with a stiletto.[5]

65. *Balarama kills the rakshasas* [Kamsa's brothers].

66. *Jarasandha* [Kamsa's father-in-law] *consoles Kamsa's wives.*

67. *Balarama and Krishna crown Ugrasena.*

At the centre of the tableau sits Ugrasena, the former ruler of Mathura deposed by his son, Kamsa.

68. *Balarama and Sri Krishnasvami straighten Kubja.*

The meeting of Krishna and the hunchback Kubja occurs at the brothers' arrival in Mathura. Kubja, an old woman, bent into two and walking with a stick, has a cup of unguent which she gives to Krishna. He then places a foot on hers, lifts her chin and she instantly becomes a beautiful young woman.

69. *Balarama and Sri Krishnasvami go to study with Sandipa* [Sandipani].

70. *Jarasandha and Krishna fighting; Jarasandha's forces; Kalayavana fights against Muchukunda; Muchukunda kills Kalayavana.* (fig. 70)

Fig. 70

After Kamsa's death, Krishna and Balarama face Jarasandha. Once Jarasandha's attacks to Mathura were repelled, yet another foe, Kalayavana, appeared at the gates of Mathura. These incidents are depicted immediately to the right of the central tableau.

In the first scene, Jarasandha, mounted on a chariot drawn by horses, sends a volley of arrows against Krishna, who, fighting on foot, valiantly repels the attack. A group of diminutive warriors, most of whom have *rakshasas'* faces, armed with swords, bucklers, tridents and spears run away.

The second scene depicts Kalayavana, dressed in outlandish garb, European-looking hat, trousers and shoes with upturned point, who armed with sword and buckler pursues Krishna. The latter, brandishing his flute, runs away from Kalayavana and lures him into a cave.

The last scene of this sequence shows King Muchukunda lying fast asleep in the cave. The arrival of Kalayavana wakes him up and a tongue of fire emanates from his eyes killing the intruder. The latter falls backwards, still brandishing his sword and buckler.

71. *Sri Krishnasvami manifests himself to Muchukunda.*

72. *Rukminidevi speaks to a Brahmin.*

This episode refers to Rukmini's elopement and subsequent wedding with Krishna.

73. *Wedding music is played. Sri Krishnasvami marries Rukminidevi.*
Label: *Brahmin.*

74. *Satrajit talks to Krishna.*

75. The story of the *syamantaka* gem.[6] (fig. 75)
Labels: *Bhadardulu (?); Prabhajat* (Prasena); *lion.*

Prabhajat, armed with a long spear, rides on a horse and attacks a lion. The animal looks like a *yali*, with a thin waist, strong hind legs, a foliated tail and a ruffled mane around its long snout. The king is accompanied by a group of four Bedas, armed with spear and one of them with a dog on the leash. Interestingly, the group of Bedas and the group of *rakshasas* accompanying Jarasandha are placed exactly on the opposite side of the central rosette.

Fig. 75

76. *Satrajit speaks to the Brahmins.*

77. **Labels:** *Jambavati kanya* [daughter of Jambavan]; *Sri Krishnasvami; Sri Krishnasvami; Jambavan.*

On the left, the daughter of Jambavan sits on a throne beneath a *pankha* (?) gently pulled by a servant standing behind her. Opposite her is Krishna with a flower in his hand. On the right, Krishna fights with Jambavan. While Jambavan uses his fists to repulse Krishna's attack, Krishna uses his flute as a weapon.

78. **Labels:** *Sri Krishnasvami; kanya* [girl]; *Jambavan; Balarama.*

Krishna reveals his divine form to Jambavan and Jambavati. Both pay homage to the god.

79. **Labels:** *Sri Krishnulu; Narakasuravadha.*

Krishna and Satyabhama, mounted on Garuda, fight against Narakasura.

80. *Srimad Narayana protects Gajendra.*
Label: *This is Gajendra.*

While the elephants frolic in the water, a ferocious crocodile has caught the leg of Gajendra. The king of the elephants, unable to get his food, gets thinner and thinner and gradually sinks in the water of the lake. He invokes Vishnu, and immediately Vishnu's *chakra* decapitates the crocodile. To the right, Vishnu places his lower right hand on Gajendra's forehead, blesses him. To the left of Vishnu is Sri Lakshmi.

81. Labels: *Satyabhama; Murahaka* [?].

82. Labels: *Sri Krishnasvami; Satyabhama.*

Krishna and Satyabhama sit on a bed. Satyabhama feeds Krishna a sweet (?) or a *pan*, while he plays with her head-jewel. A shower of flowers enlivens the background.

83. Labels: *Rakshasas; Churning the Milk Ocean.*

Four *asuras* and three *devas* hold respectively the head and the tail of the six-hooded snake, Vasuki. The two groups stand in the ocean, suggested by a rippling blue band teeming with fish and shells. At the centre of the tableau is Vishnu in his incarnation as Kurma, supporting Mount Mandara around which the snake's body is coiled. The Mandara is seen from a bird's view perspective, so as to effectively show the coiled snake's body wound around it.

Central rosette

84. *Sri Krishnasvami and his eight wives.*

Notes

1. Verghese 2000: 292–302, Dallapiccola 2010: 232–235.
2. It should really be a *chakra*. This motif is still very popular in Odisha.
3. This theme appears in South Indian sculpture in the Chola period, and is particularly popular from the 15th century onwards.
4. *Bhagavata Purana* X, 23.
5. According to the *Bhagavata Purana* X, 44.36–38, Krishna grabs Kamsa by the hair and hurls him down from the high dais to the ground of the arena, thus killing him. There is, however, another tradition, according to which Krishna enters Kamsa's palace and kills him. The latter seems to be popular in South India. (See Dallapiccola 2010: 72, cat. no. 4.93.)
6. Krishna had asked Satrajit to present the jewel to Ugrasena, the Yadava king, but Satrajit refused to do so. Prabhajat, one of the sons of Satrajit, who wore the *syamantaka* around the neck, was killed by a lion while hunting. The lion was killed by Jambavan, and the latter took the *syamantaka*, and gave it to his children to play with. When Prabhajat did not return home, there was a rumour that Krishna had killed Prabhajat and stolen the gem (no. 75). Krishna went to the forest in search of the gem and found it in Jambavan's cave. A fight ensued between Krishna and Jambavan (no. 77). Eventually Jambavan—who in the past had been one of Rama's allies—realized that his opponent was none other than Vishnu himself, sought his blessing, offering him not only the *syamantaka* jewel but also his daughter Jambavati in marriage (no. 78).

Two Episodes from the *Mahabharata* (cat. 10–11)

These two *kalamkaris* from the Madurai area illustrate two of the most dramatic episodes of the *Mahabharata*: the killing of Shishupala[1] and the duel between the two arch-rivals, Arjuna and Karna.[2] Dispensing with the central tableau, both narratives are laid out in four registers. The Shishupala narrative (cat. 10) reaches its climax in the third register, when Krishna decapitates Shishupala. Despite this incident, Dharmaraja's, i.e. Yudhishthira's, coronation rituals continue and once completed, the Brahmins who officiated receive gifts and donations (nos. 8 and 9).

The layout of cat. 11, depicting the final contest between Arjuna and Karna, is similar to that of cat. 7. In both hangings the registers are divided by a narrow band enlivened by red dots; white rosettes dot the red background. The scenes flow one into the other without solution of continuity and bear brief explanatory captions in Tamil.

Notes

1. *Mahabharata, Sabha parvan*, ch. 26.
2. *Mahabharata, Karna parvan*, ch. 90–91.

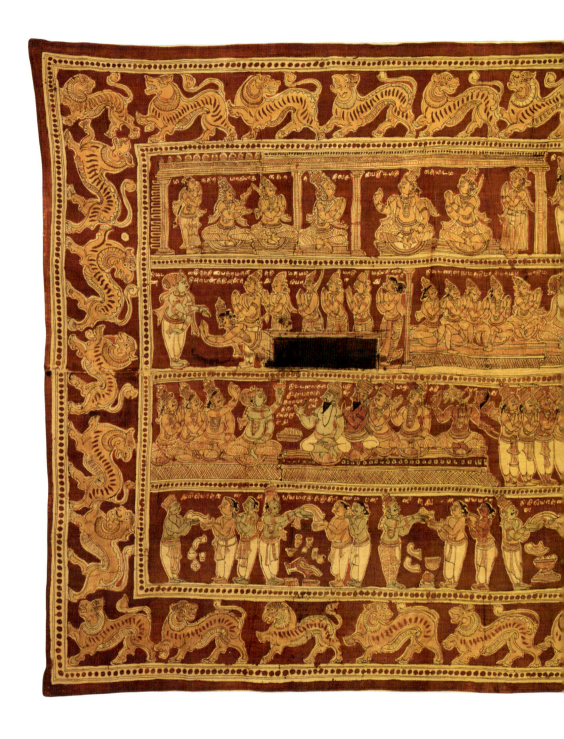

The Killing of Shishupala MADURAI

10

The Killing of Shishupala Madurai

The deep hatred Shishupala felt for Krishna goes back to his previous lives: in one of them he was Hiranyakashipu, who eventually was disembowelled by Vishnu in his incarnation as Narasimha; in another he was the mighty Ravana, killed by Vishnu in his Rama *avatara*. Eventually, he was born into the royal Chedi family as Shishupala.

Shishupala and Krishna met face to face at Dharmaraja's coronation. He objected strongly to Krishna's presence at the ceremony, as the latter was not a king. In his wrath, Shishupala rose to leave the assembly taking with him a number of other kings, but was recalled by Dharmaraja. He then decided to disrupt the ceremony, and eventually, after having heaped upon Krishna all kind of insults, he challenged him. Krishna then brandished his *chakra*, threw it at Shishupala, decapitating him (fig. 6). At that moment a divine radiance emanated from the dead body and merged into Krishna's. After Shishupala's funerary rites, however, Dharmaraja's consecration was concluded.

The narrative illustrated in this *kalamkari* commences with the invitation and the arrival of Krishna at the court of the Pandavas, culminates with the killing of Shishupala, and ends with the completion of Dharmaraja's coronation, followed by the distribution of gifts to the Brahmins and Krishna's return to Dvarka.

10. The Killing of Shishupala
5459 (IS)
Dimensions: 192 x 270 cm
Date: 19th century
Provenance: Madurai region
Captions: in Tamil

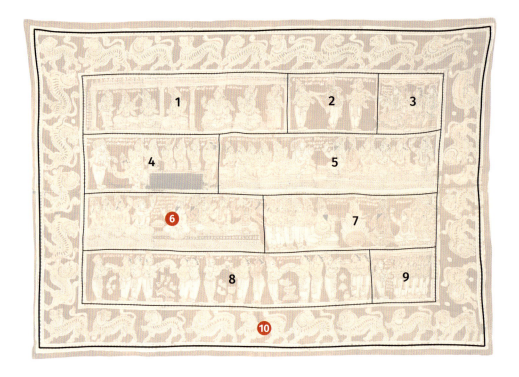

CAPTIONS

Top register

1. *The town of Indraprastha; the court gathered at Indraprastha.*

2. and 3. *A letter of invitation was sent from the court to Sri Krishnasvami; Sri Krishnasvami received the letter of invitation and read it.*

Second register

4. *Dharmaraja and his brothers welcome Sri Krishnasvami into the palace.*

5. *Dharmaraja and his brothers talk to Dronacharya in secret. Krishna.*

   Although the caption states that Dharmaraja talks to Dronacharya in secret, it is Krishna, at the centre of the composition, that talks to the sage seated opposite him. At Krishna's side are the five Pandavas. Behind Dronacharya are Bhishma and four crowned Kauravas.

Third register

6. *While Sri Krishnasvami was in the assembly hall, he throws the plate* [i.e. the *chakra*] *at Shishupala.* (fig. 6)

   To the left, Krishna sits along with three Pandavas; opposite him, on a similar *asana* are Dronacharya, Bhishma, two Kaurava princes and Shishupala. Between the two groups is a tray or a container with materials for the imminent sacrifice. It is clear from their body language that they are involved in a violent argument. At this point, Krishna lets loose his redoubtable *chakra* and decapitates Shishupala, whose head is falling to the ground while sinews and blood spill out of his severed neck.

Fig. 6

7. *Dronacharya and Bhishmacharya performing a yaga; Krishna.*

Fourth register

8. *Duryodhana gives presents to the Brahmins.*

    At the end of the ceremonies, Duryodhana—according to the caption, but probably this is an error of the scribe for Dharmaraja—distributes various gifts to the Brahmins.

9. *Krishna returns to Dvarka.*

Border

On all four sides are playful lions (fig. 10), and at the centre of the right border is a *hamsa*.

Fig. 10   *Bottom border*

The Duel between Karna and Arjuna
MADURAI

11 The Duel between Karna and Arjuna **Madurai**

Karna was son of Surya and Kunti, who, to conceal her premarital affair, abandoned the child at birth. He was adopted by a childless family of humble origins. In due course, the boy was sent to the capital city of the Pandavas and was brought up with his half-brothers. While learning archery Arjuna and Karna vied with each other; their rivalry increased with the passing of time and, after completing his education, Karna sided with the Kauravas. Before the war between the Pandavas and the Kauravas started, Kunti went alone to meet Karna. She revealed to him that she was his mother and that the Pandavas were his half-brothers. She tried to persuade Karna to join the Pandavas, but he refused, promising her that he would kill Arjuna on the battlefield, but spare his four remaining brothers.

This *kalamkari* depicts the last duel between Karna and Arjuna. In the first register the two antagonists seated in their war chariots (fig. 1) drive to the battlefield preceded by the infantry and cavalry (fig. 9). In the second and third registers the battle continues unabated among the carnage: human and animal limbs are strewn on the battlefield, chariots are destroyed, warriors maimed, while all kinds of missiles crisscross in the background. In the fourth, Arjuna faces Karna, and kills him.

11. The Duel between Karna and Arjuna
IM 28-1911

Dimensions: 193 x 277 cm
Date: 19th century
Provenance: Madurai region
Captions: in Tamil

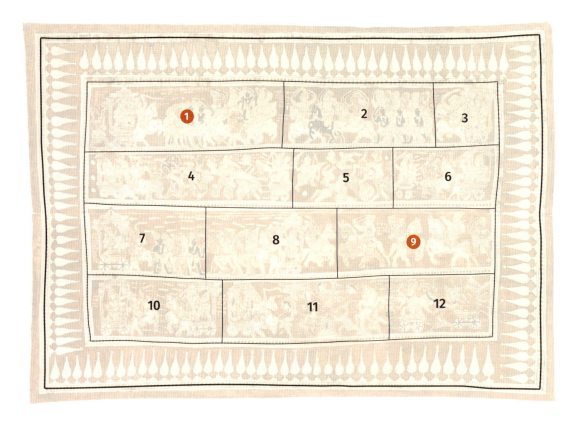

CAPTIONS

Top register

1. *Arjuna goes to battle; Arjuna and his army.* (fig. 1)

   On the left, preceded by a group of six men and five horsemen: Arjuna, on a war chariot, proceeds towards the battlefield aiming arrows at his enemy.

   Fig. 1

2. *Battle between Arjuna and Karna maharaja.*

3. *Karna and his big army on the march.*

Second register

4. *The place where Karna and Arjuna fought against each other.*

5. *The centre of the register depicts Karna on foot.*

   His crown has been shot away by an arrow and he proceeds towards Arjuna among the carnage of the battlefield.

6. *Arjuna aims his arrows.*

Third register

7. *Arjuna shoots his arrows.*

8. *Arjuna's army fight against Karna's army.*

9. *The cavalry.* (fig. 9)

Fig. 9

The right half of this register illustrates a fight between horsemen armed with swords and bucklers. Behind the last horseman is a footman armed with sword.

Fourth register

10. *Arjuna.*

11. *The duel between Karna and Arjuna.*

    The central and the right portion of this register illustrate the final battle between Arjuna and Karna. On the battlefield are severed limbs, broken weapons, animal carcasses and chariot debris. Soldiers die transfixed by arrows and fall to the ground still holding their weapons. At the centre of the scene the body of a decapitated warrior falls to the ground. A horse hit by an arrow baulks up, its mouth wide open.

12. *Arjuna shoots his arrows.*

    The two adversaries face one another. Eventually, Karna's chariot is destroyed; hit by Arjuna's arrow, the hero falls to the ground.

Borders

The borders display a very sober pattern constituted by elongated vase-shaped elements as in cat. 18.

Two Ganga Hangings (cat. 12–13)

These two cloths illustrate episodes drawn from the *Katamaraju Katha*,[1] 'The story of Katamaraju', a narrative genealogy of the most important herding community of Andhra and Telangana, the Gollas, or Yadavas. These hangings, used in the performance of the epic, focus on the exploits of Katamaraju, its main hero, deemed to be an incarnation of Krishna and of his immediate predecessors.

The *Katamaraju Katha* is based on the conflict between the nomadic Gollas and the sedentary agricultural communities. The Gollas and their cattle moved in different areas of today's Telangana and Andhra Pradesh. Katamaraju brought his herds into the territory of the king of Nellore, and requested grazing rights from him. Manumasiddhi, who ruled the area of Nellore in the 13th century, was a contemporary of the Kakatiya ruler Prataparudra (r. 1289–1323). The causes of the conflict between Manumasiddhi—Nallasiddhi or Siddhiraju, as he is called in the hangings—and the Gollas are not clear. According to an inscription which contains a version of the story, it was caused by Katamaraju's refusal to pay the grazing tax due to the king.[2]

Although the cycle is named after its main hero, the goddess Gangamma, or Yadava Gangamma, the tutelary deity of the Gollas, shown in the central panel of both hangings, is the most important figure of the epic which is performed 'as a mode of worshiping her'.[3] By sponsoring the performances of the *Katamaraju Katha* and supporting the performers, the Gollas celebrate their lineage, their glorious past, thus firmly establishing their identity in a grand way.

Gangamma, the tutelary deity of the Gollas, is one of the many village deities of peninsular India. As her name, Ganga, i.e. 'swift-flowing', suggests, she "shares not only the name but also characteristics of the pan-Indian river goddess, Ganga—fluidity and potentially destructive force or *shakti*."[4] The vital importance of the water, especially when the drought leads to Katamaraju's fight with Nallasiddhi, is one of the main motifs of the epic.[5] Nowadays, apart from the Gollas, Gangamma is worshipped also by a number of other communities in the Prakasam district of Andhra Pradesh, particularly at Donakonda in Darsi *taluka*.

Performing traditions

The *Katamaraju Katha* is performed in many different ways by the various communities of singers. The most renowned of the Andhra performing traditions is that of the Kommulavallu or Kommulavaru, a Dalit community, who are hired by the Gollas to perform the ballads at the Ganga *jatra* [festival]. They are said to be the descendants of Birnidu, one of the brave Dalit warriors who fought on Katamaraju's side. Bhaktiranna, the sole relative of Katamaraju to survive the battle against Nallasiddhi at Yerragaddapadu, ordained the sons of Birnidu to sing the glory of his ancestors and maintain the family records of the Yadava heroes. This is why these minstrels are patronized by all the Yadava communities throughout Telangana and Andhra Pradesh, particularly in the southern parts of Coastal Andhra.[6]

In the districts of Guntur and Prakasam, the Kommus[7] are called *Gudaralu*, from *gudaram*, tent, because they erect a tent in which they hang large paintings, of Gangamma and of Katamaraju, and sing the stories.

Unlike the other great Telugu epic, the *Palnadi Virula Katha*,[8] no systematic research has been undertaken on the story of Katamaraju, and thus most of the ballads are unknown to the scholarly world.[9]

Furthermore, the singers perform only sections of this huge work, so it is probable that some parts of the cycle are no longer known.[10] This explains why the hangings, known locally as Ganga *duppati* [blanket], do not seem to follow a chronologically consistent story line, but are a collection of different incidents involving the main characters of the epic, their relatives, and allies.

The events narrated in the *Katamaraju Katha*, in particular the climactic Yerragaddapadu battle, date probably from the last quarter of the 13th century. The borders between myth and history are blurred: the epic traces the ancestry of its main hero back to Krishna, but sources differ with one another regarding the number of generations which lived between Krishna and Katamaraju. However, the last three generations consisting of Avula Valuraju (also called Avularaju), Peddiraju, and Katamaraju are not disputed by any source. The historicity of these three chiefs in succession can be corroborated by epigraphic and other literary sources.[11]

The stories (*the numbers in brackets refer to the episodes illustrated in cat. 12*)
The narrative covers three generations of Golla chiefs culminating in the battle of Yerragaddapadu, in which both Katamaraju and his adversary Nallasiddhi, as well as their followers, died.

The Golla chiefs were originally settled in the region of Yelamanchili (Elamanchili), in what is now Vishakapatnam district. According to the narrative, they first moved westwards and later migrated southwards.[12]

Avula Valuraju was the Golla chief of Yelamanchili. He had five sons and one daughter. Before his death in battle, he arranged for his second son, Peddiraju, to succeed him. Peddiraju ruled Yelamanchili for about ten years and then moved with his brothers to Pampadri where he ruled for further seven years. Since he had no children he divided his property of cows, gold, jewellery and other valuables among his brothers and sister (nos. 10, 12), and left for Kalyananagara, today's Basavakalyan in Bidar district, Karnataka. There, he worshipped Someshvara, and by divine intervention, he had a son, Katamaraju, and a daughter, Papanuka (fig. 6).Eventually, Peddiraju died fighting his enemy, King Valiketuvaraju. Katamaraju, then a seven-year-old boy, went to the battlefield at night to look for his father's body. There, for the first time, he met the goddess Gangamma who fell in love with him and was very keen on marrying him. Katamaraju managed to extricate himself from his difficult position. He then proceeded to the battlefield and there he confronted Ganga's younger brother, Poturaju, a demon who devours corpses. He overcame Poturaju, decapitated King Valiketuvaraju (no. 31) and brought the body of his father back home. Peddiraju's wife, Peddamma, committed *sati* on the body of her husband, leaving their children orphaned (no. 26).

Since all of Peddiraju's brothers had died fighting, Bhaktiranna, also known as Battiranna, one of Peddiraju's nephews, brought Katamaraju and Papanuka back to his capital, Donakonda, where they were looked after by his mother, Sridevi. Eventually, Katamaraju ascended the throne at Yelamanchili.[13] Later, Katamaraju moved with his cattle herds to the region of Srisailam; then, on advice of Gangamma, he migrated towards the fertile region of Nellore ruled by Nallasiddhi. Some kinsmen had warned Katamaraju not to go towards Nellore because Mukkanti, a chieftain of Nellore, had killed his uncle Poluraju. Despite the warning, Katamaraju entered an agreement with

Nallasiddhi on the payment of the *pullari* or grazing tax which, eventually, led to fresh trouble between Katamaraju and Nallasiddhi.[14] In the violent battle that followed, Katamaraju killed Nallasiddhi, avenged the death of his uncle but he also succumbed to his injuries in the war.

At the time of the decisive battle of Yerragaddapadu, Bhaktiranna (figs. 6–7) was on a pilgrimage to Kashi. While he was there he heard the news of the death of Katamaraju and his own brothers. He returned at once to Donakonda to perform the death rituals for his deceased relatives on the banks of the River Paleru.

This is the outline of the main narrative, which is interwoven with a wealth of sub-stories detailing the life and adventures of the heroes on both sides of the conflict.

Katamaraju and Gangamma (cat. 12.39)
Gangamma's elusive presence dominates the whole epic; her relationship with Katamaraju is ambiguous from their first encounter at night in the battlefield. Although the goddess is keen on marrying the young hero, he finds various excuses to postpone the wedding. Eventually, when the wedding is celebrated, the bride appears before Katamaraju in her real divine aspect. Katamaraju recognizes her: she is the same person he met as a young boy at night on the battlefield. The marriage is concluded, but the hero maintains his celibate status and never lives with his bride.[15]

The singers explain this difficult relationship as a consequence of the prior identities of both Katamaraju and his bride. With an ingenious re-telling of the famous story of the exchange of babies from the *Bhagavata Purana* the singers demonstrate that Katamaraju is an *avatara* of Krishna, and the goddess is Yasodha's daughter, reborn as Gangamma. According to the story, Vasudeva placed Krishna by the side of Yasodha and took her newly born daughter away. Once back in Mathura, he handed the baby over to Kamsa (see cat. 9.15–9.18). When the latter was on the point of killing her, she revealed her true identity as Mayadevi. Mayadevi was eventually born as Gangamma, while Krishna was born as Katamaraju: they are thus brother and sister. This unresolved tension permeates their whole relationship.[16]

Notes

1. The oldest and, possibly, longest cycle of ballads in the Telugu oral tradition of Andhra after the *Palnadi Virula Katha*, the 'Epic of Palnadu'.
2. Talbot 2001: 77
3. Claus 2003: 329.
4. Burkhalter Fluckiger 2013: 7.
5. Narayana Rao 1986: 144.
6. Nagabhushana Sarma 1995: 37–38.
7. The name Kommu is derived from the brass horn-shaped wind instrument, *kommu*, which the Kommulavaru play during their performances
8. Roghair 1982.
9. Only about 20 stories/ballads have been collected by T.V. Subba Rao in the years 1963–68 and have been published in his *Kathamaraju Kathalu*, 2 vols., Haidarabadu, Andhra Pradesh Sahitya Akademi, 1976 and 1977.
10. Subba Rao 2001: 191–192.
11. Sadanandam 2008: 132.
12. Sadanandam 2008: 130–131.
13. Sadanandam 2008: 131.
14. For details on the agreement between Nallasiddhi and Katamaraju, see Narayana Rao 1989: 105–121.
15. "He thinks of her as his mother, the great goddess. He conceives of the thread on his wrist … as a band signifying a vow to kill his enemies rather than a band for his marriage vows, and pours the rice on her head as an act of worship rather than as a ritual act of marrying. He makes an announcement that he is not going to untie the band on his wrist until he has defeated his enemies." (Narayana Rao 1989: 108).
16. Narayana Rao 1989: 110–111.

Ganga Duppati MACHILIPATNAM

This cloth was prepared by the master dyer Panchakalla Pedda Subbarayudu:[1] his signature, the date, and the place where this work was executed are in the caption beneath the central image of the goddess Gangamma.

The narrative is laid out on nine registers. Vaishnava imagery occurs throughout the hanging: in the upper row are Anjaneya (Hanuman) carrying the mountain (no. 3), and Garuda (no. 5). Vira Anjaneya being worshipped by two warriors is on row five (fig. 19). Since Katamaraju is deemed to be an *avatara* of Krishna, episodes from the *Krishnacharita* also appear: Yasodha breastfeeding Krishna (no. 16), Kalingamardana (no. 20), Putanavadha (no. 21), Venugopala (no. 22), love scene (no. 23), and Gopikavastraharana (no. 24). Finally, Krishna lifting Mount Govardhana appears in the left spandrel (no. 40) of the central tableau. A rendering of the Churning of the Milk Ocean (no. 36) is at the centre of the last register.

Apart from the central tableau, the goddess appears in few other scenes, in no. 5, near Garuda, and in no. 31 when Katamaraju kills King Valiketuvaraju. Scenes of worship occur in nos. 12 and 38. The *jatra* (festival) depicted here, may possibly be the famous Donakonda *jatra*, which takes place in the month of *Chaitra*, i.e. March/April, complete with animal sacrifice, hook-swinging, and mounds of rice.

The palette is very limited: the main colours are various shades of red, beige and black. Except for the large icon of Gangamma at the centre of the hanging, in which every detail has been carefully drawn, the depiction of the figures is kept as simple as possible.

A set of stencils has been used to draw the characters. Each stencil has been used for all the similar characters (fig. 2), with minimal variations in the pattern of their costumes, jewellery and headgear.

As already suggested, the choice of scenes shown on the textiles is probably determined by the singers' repertoire. No systematic research has been undertaken on the story of Katamaraju, hence the identification of the various episodes illustrated in both cat. 12 and cat. 13 is, at best, tentative.

KALAMKARI TEMPLE HANGINGS

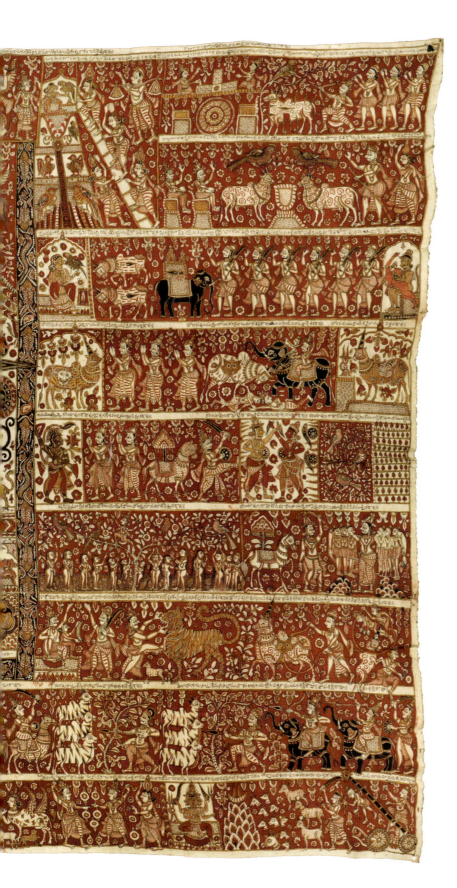

12. Ganga *duppati*[2]
2102-1883 (IS)
Dimensions: 294 x 419 cm
Date: 1881/82
Provenance: Bandaru (Machilipatnam)
Artist: Panchakalla Pedda Subbarayudu
Captions: in Telugu

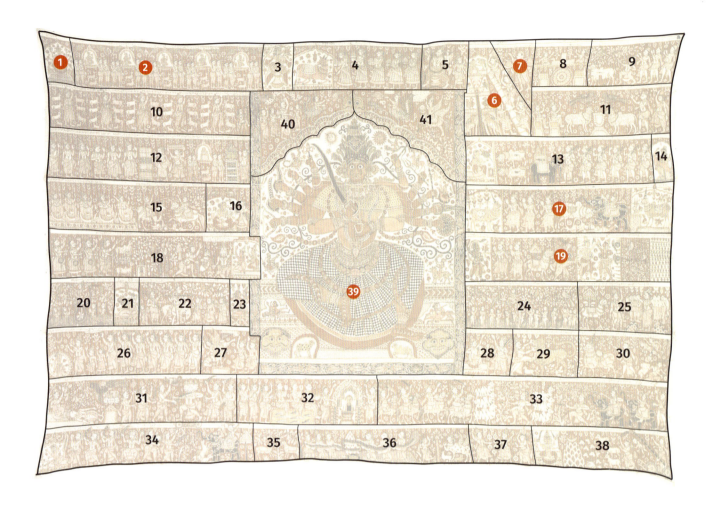

CAPTIONS

First register

Fig. 1

1. *Vinayaka* [Ganesha].[3] (fig. 1)

2. *Yeranukaraju; Simhadriraju is going to Gavirikonda, Nalanukaraju to Vijayavada, Poluraju to Chilkamarri; Peddiraju is on the way to Kalyani.* (fig. 2)

   Peddiraju and his brothers, the father and uncles of Katamaraju, having left Pampadri, travel to different destinations. Peddiraju, and his wife, Peddamma, the future parents of Katamaraju and Papanuka, will eventually settle in Kalyani. **(see cat.13.30)**

3. *Anjaneya (Hanuman) brings the mountain.*[4]

12 **Ganga Duppati** Machilipatnam

Fig. 2

4. *Pampadri Basavanna and the five daughters-in-law* [of Avularaju], *Simhadri Sita, Yeranuka Sita, Nalanuka Sita, Sridevi* [the fifth name, i.e. Peddamma Devi, is missing].

   Except Peddiraju, all his brothers had children. When his wife, Peddamma, reverently touches the bull's anterior hoof, the animal turns his head in the opposite direction, rejecting her offering, as she has no offspring.[5] **(see cat. 13.7)**

5. *Garudalvar kills the snake.*

   To Garuda's left is a smaller four-armed figure, probably Devi. The disposition of the icon of Pampadri Basavanna, between Ajnaneya and Garudalvar (Garuda), followed by a diminutive Devi image, suggests the connection between the Gollas, who are descendants of Krishna, hence Vaishnavas, with Devi, who plays a major role both in Krishna's and in Katamaraju's life.

6. *Papanuka has been confined on top of a pillar.* (fig. 6)

   Once in Kalyani, Peddiraju and his wife, Peddamma, worshipped Someshvara [Shiva] and in due course Katamaraju and his sister Papanuka were born. Papanuka was born under an unlucky star; shortly after her birth, Peddiraju died in battle against King Valiketuvaraju (or Ketuvaraju; see no. 31). Peddamma, then, performed *sati*. On his way to Kashi, Bhaktiranna (Bhattiranna) found his orphaned cousins Katamaraju and Papanuka in Kalyani, and placed them under the care of his mother, Sridevi, in Donakonda.[6] Because of her inauspicious birth chart, Papanuka was confined by her aunt, Sridevi, in a palace built on a single pillar, outside the town. **(see cat. 13.3)**

7. [On the top border] *Bhattiranna carries the annakavadi* [a yoke onto which two containers with food are suspended]. (fig. 7)

   Bhaktiranna (Bhattiranna), the elder son of one of Peddiraju's brothers and Sridevi, is on his way to Kashi. **(see cat. 13.4)**

Fig. 6 Fig. 7

139

8. [Illegible] *Katamaraju and Padmanaidu* [Katamaraju's uncle] *play chess on the board* [illegible] *in Jannivada;* [beneath the board game scene] *They are playing chess on the board.*

   The scene is divided into two horizontal sections. On the top, two crowned figures, Katamaraju and Padmanaidu (Katamaraju's uncle; he is also known as Papi Nayudu), sit facing each other across a *pachisi* board. The lower part of the scene is occupied by an elaborate floral motif at the centre flanked by empty thrones. **(see cat. 13.5)**

9. *At Yerragaddapadu he gets all the arrows* [illegible] *Padmanaidu applauds* [?]. (see cat. 13.34)

Second register

10. *Yeranukaraju is dividing the cows; Simhadriraju dividing the cows; Nalanukaraju is dividing the cows; Poluraju is dividing the cows; Peddiraju is dividing the cows; This man seduces a woman.*

    This episode refers to events prior to the birth of Katamaraju. After having ruled Pampadri for seven years along with his brothers, the childless Peddiraju divided his property among his brothers and sister, Komarakka (or Komaramma), and left for Kalyani. **(see cat. 13.28)**

11. *Katamaraju and Padmanaidu go* [illegible]; *they pour milk in a trough for the cows to drink. Katamaraju sends earrings to Kondamma (Komarakka); a shepherdess carries milk for the cattle.*
    (see cat. 13.35)

Third register

12. *Yeranukaraju, Simhadriraju, Nalanukkaraju, Poluraju, Peddiraju. The sons-in-law share the money; Komarakka carries the box with the money; Komarakka places the box on the palanquin and takes it away; worship of Gangadevi.*

    The riches to be shared are piled up in boxes. Komarakka chooses her box. It is the heaviest and contains an image of the goddess Durga. Her brothers give her a large sum of cash to meet the expenses to worship the deity. In the last scene, Komarakka worships the goddess Ganga, depicted as a huge head placed on a tall pedestal.[7]
    (see cat. 13.19)

13. *Yerrayya's bulls charge Kundamadevi's tower. Kundamadevi puts an arrow on the elephant* [unclear] *and shoots arrows against the cowherds;* [illegible].

    Kundamadevi, wife of Nallasiddhi, ruler of Nellore, had a tame pet parrot. One day, the bird left the palace and flew towards the forest where the Gollas were grazing their cattle. Its shrieks disturbed the animals and Padma Raghava, a follower of

Katamaraju, shot an arrow at the bird. The wounded parrot returned to the palace and died before the queen. Kundamadevi was furious and sent some Boyas to kill the cows of the Gollas. Katamaraju, however, killed the Boyas and refused to pay the grazing tax to Nallasiddhi. (see cat. 13.11)

14. Amorous couple in an alcove.

Fourth register

15. *A fight in Ballikuravakonda: Tamballa Brahmayya and Tikkana mantri fight.*

    Before the decisive encounter of Yerragaddapadu, Nallasiddhi of Nellore sent an embassy to Katamaraju. The negotiations, however, ended in a duel with fatal outcome between Tikkanna *mantri*, a Brahmin warrior and commander-in chief of Nallasiddhi, and Tamballa Brahmayya, who was fighting on the Golla's side. (see cat. 13.12)

16. *Yasodha breastfeeds Krishnamurti.*
    (see cat. 13.13)

17. *Kadaraju (Katamaraju) and Padmanaidu talk to the cow. In the battle of Yerragaddapadu, Bolyavu stabs Siddhiraju's elephant. After the battle, the cow goes to Kailasa.* (fig. 17)

    On the second day of the battle, the Bollavu (or Bolyavu), a divine one-horned cow, caused heavy damage to Siddhiraju's (i.e. Nallasiddhi's) army, and by the close of the day it was killed by the Boyas who joined Siddhiraju. (see cat. 13.15)

Fig. 17

Fifth register

18. *Shilamradevi comes* [illegible] *Poluraju* [illegible] *to the Jangalus* [?]; *Poluraju gives the buffalos and cows to the Jangalus and sends them to the Srisailam mountain.* [Beneath the drawing]: *Poluraju asks Mukkanti* [illegible] *the Jangalus and to bring them to him* [?].

    This sequence of episodes is unclear. (see cat. 13.21)

19. *Karyavularaju* [son of Simhadri Raju], *and Pullavula Keshavanna* [son of Komarakka] *are paying homage to Hanuman; Karyavularaju attacks Bethala*

[the commander-in-chief of Prataparudra of Orugallu, formerly Warangal]; *Karyavularaju picks flowers from the garden.* (fig. 19)

(see cat. 13.17)

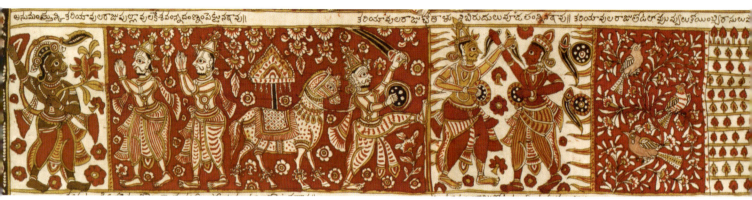

Fig. 19

Sixth register

20. *Krishnamurti quells the snake Kalinga (Kaliya).*

    For a similar layout, see also no. 24. **(see cat. 13.16)**

21. *Krishnamurti kills Putana.*

22. *Balaramasvami carries the plough; Krishnamurti plays the flute.*

23. *The [illegible] gopikas make Krishnamurti sit on their lap.*

24. *Krishnamurti steals all the clothes of the gopikas and hangs them on a tree.* **(see cat. 13.8)**

25. *Karyavularaju takes the malinas under his arms and crushes them.*

    This episode is not clear; it may illustrate an episode of the Battle of Karyavularaju.[8]

Seventh register

26. *Peddammadevi hands Katamaraju and Papanuka over to Muddamma; Battiramma is performing penance in order to have children. Mudamma is handing over seven sisters.*

    Peddamma performs *sati*: she stands with her left hand raised in a circle of flames. Opposite her is a man carrying a bell in the right hand and his left extended as if blessing her. Katamaraju, his sister Papanuka, and seven female figures, all with their right hand raised, follow the man. **(see cat. 13.14)**

27. *The winged horse carries Puttamaraju from the clouds [to earth].*

    Cartouche on the painting: *Throwing him* [illegible]...

    Puttamaraju [son of Komaramma, and husband of Agumanchi] descends from the sky riding his winged horse and brandishing his whip. He is depicted again, in no. 41.

28. *Kalarimaranna brings a letter [?] and gives it to Ajitamaraju's daughter, Singiribogalli, and she reads it.*

On the leaf: *'May you be successful'*. **(see cat. 13.18)**

29. *Kuppokondanna fights against the tiger and rips its mouth apart.*
(see cat. 13.6)

30. *They catch the cow* [Bolyavu, the one-horned cow] *with ropes, and chain her, but she turns back and stabs them.*

Eighth register

31. *Peddiraju lies down beneath a gangaregi tree; the eagle brings Ketuvaraju's heads and drops them at the feet of Peddiraju; Poturaju, Ganga and Katamaraju cut off the heads of Ketuvaraju. Bhumi Ketuvaraju; Nili Ketuvaraju.*

The correct sequence of the scenes is unclear; probably, this depicts the first encounter of the seven-year old Katamaraju and the goddess Ganga. Katamaraju goes to the battlefield at night to recover the body of his father, Peddiraju. There he encounters the goddess Gangamma and her brother, Poturaju. The goddess falls in love and wants to marry him. **(see cat. 13.14)**

32. *Agumanchi* [daughter of Poluraju]; *Komaramma* [sister of Peddiraju and mother of Puttamaraju]; *Sridevi* [wife of Poluraju]; *Puttamaraju* [husband of Agumanchi]; *Pallikonda* [adopted son of Komaramma]; *Aithamaraju* [son of Sridevi]; *Chemburungudi* [temple around which the tree is grown]. *They cut the plant; they are going on a pilgrimage.*

This sequence is unclear. The object of devotion is a *mukhalinga* flanked by two arrowheads in a shrine surrounded by a creeper which is cut down with axes by two youths.

33. *Sellapinnaya; Padmanaidu; Katamaraju;* [illegible]; *Modubulu attacks the cattle; Yarasiddhiraju; Papasiddhiraju; Palasiddhiraju.*

Possibly this refers to one of the encounters of the Gollas and Nallasiddhi's Boyas before the final battle.

34. *Viranayudu is performing Shiva puja and paying homage to the sword; Viranayudu blows the horn and dances; clapping the hands; cutting the tree; Viranayudu's dogs bite Siddhiraju's elephant.*

The first scene may refer to the *katti-seva*, sword-play as a form of worship, which leads to a kind of spirit possession.[9] **(see cat. 13.31)**

35. *Mummaya* [son of Poluraju and Sridevi] *and Pochayya* [adoptive son of Agumanchi and of her husband Puttamaraju] *tie the rams to the tree.*
(see cat. 13.32)

36. *Devatas and rakshasas churn the Milk Ocean with the Mandaragiri parvatam [Mount Mandara] to get the Amrita; they get Mahalakshmi, Kalpavriksha and Kamadhenu; they are all talking.*
(see cat. 13.23)

37. *Mummaya and Posaya [Pochayya] play with the tops and the top hits the girl's foot.*[10]
(see cat. 13.33)

38. *They pour four pots of atirasa; the goats have been sacrificed; Balarama climbs the pole.*

Gangamma in a shrine; goats' heads are scattered all around.[11] The last scene is a depiction of the *chidi mari*, hook swinging. **(see cat. 13.36–13.37)**

39. *In the year Vrisha (i.e. 1881/82) in the month of Chaitra (i.e. March/April) on Saturday. Panchakalla Pedda Subbarayudu, who lived in Bandaru [Machilipatnam] wrote the whole story of the Yadavas on a Ganga sari and boiled it with the kalamkari root.* (fig. 39)

Beneath a lobed arch, the red-complexioned, twelve-armed goddess Gangamma sits on a throne. Her face is dominated by her awe-inspiring, reddened eyes. On her forehead is a horizontal *tilaka*. She wears a blouse and her typical black-and-white chequered skirt adorned by three elaborate girdles. Her hair is carefully tied in a complex *jatamakuta* adorned by four snakes, two on each side, and two peacock's feathers. The top of the *makuta* is embellished by a flower and by a small winding creeper, and flanked by the sun and the moon. Six *nathas*, all blowing a horn and riding on diverse animals, are accommodated among the creeper and her arms surround her.

Fig. 39

From left to right, they ride: a fish, a scorpion, a snake, a deer (?), a tortoise, and a tiger. To the left and the right, beneath her knees, are amorous couples, and on either side on the base of her *asana* are a *kirttimukha* (?) and a cow. All around the image is a river, the Paleru, flowing near the Ganga temple in Donakonda.

According to the singers, after the battle at Yerragaddapadu, the Gollas returned to Donakonda and cleaned their weapons in the Paleru and buried their weapons within the temple precincts. Battiranna, the sole survivor of the line, is believed to have performed the last rites for the dead on the banks of this stream. Donakonda is therefore a crucial place in Golla tradition and the goddess is known as Donakonda Ganga.[12] **(see cat. 13.44)**

40. *Krishna Govardhanadhara.*

The caption is written on Mount Govardhana, imaginatively rendered as a scroll-like shape with four peaks. Immediately to the right of Krishna is a *kinnari*. The same motif is repeated again on the spandrel to the right, near the *kirttimukha* mask. The label reads: *amsakanya* (i.e. half-girl). **(see cat. 13.26)**

41. *Puttamaraju is carried by a winged horse and is armed with a weapon called Gangabalyan.*

Puttamaraju subdued the wild horse of Prataparudra, ruler of Orugallu.

Notes

1. The same artist is responsible for the Ramayana canopy (cat. 1) and the Mahalakshmi *pithakam* (cat. 14).
2. '*Duppati*' means blanket, a long, usually thick cloth to cover the body with, or to be used as a bedspread. It might also be used as a prop to narrate the story. Personal communication by Prof. V. Narayana Rao, 16 July 2013.
3. Vaishnava attributes in Ganesha's upper hands are features typical of some of the Andhra *kalamkaris*, e.g. Srikalahasti.
4. Two major aspects of Anjaneya are combined here: Vira Anjaneya, a very popular form of Anjaneya in Andhra Pradesh, Telangana and Karnataka, and the *Ramayana* episode in which Anjaneya carries the mountain with the healing herbs. (see cat. 5.42).
5. Narayana Rao 1989: 109–110.
6. Present-day Ganga Donakonda in Prakasam dist., Andhra Pradesh.
7. Narayana Rao 1989: 110
8. Subba Rao 2001: 191 d.
9. *Katti-seva* is an important ritual of the Hero Cult of Palnadu. "Katti-seva is most commonly performed by Malas but members of other castes also take their turns. Thurston (1975 [1909] vol. II: 295) has observed the same kind of ritual among the Gollas. He spoke of the person performing Katti-seva as having been possessed by the spirit of an ancestor. The same ancestor is recognizable as a character in another Telugu epic tradition Katama Raju Katha." (Roghair 1982: 29).
10. The meaning of this episode is not clear. Subba Rao notes a recurring motif: a young hero plays tops unaware of the battle being fought by his father. Is the Komati girl depicted here predicting the fatal outcome of the battle? (Subba Rao 2001: 196; motif 17)
11. For a description of Gangamma *puja*, see Thurston and Rangachari vol. II: 294–295.
12. Sadanandam 2008: 139.

Ganga Duppati MACHILIPATNAM

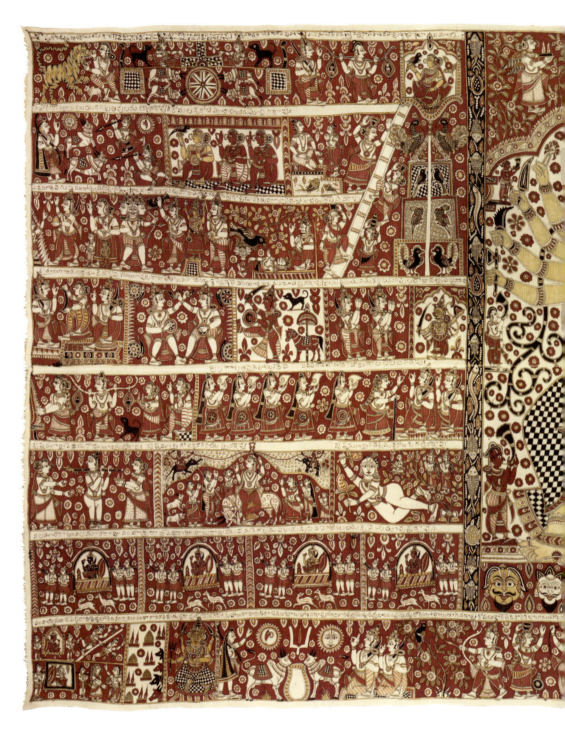

13 **Ganga Duppati** Machilipatnam

13. Ganga *duppati*[1]
1759-1883 (IS)
Dimensions: 195 x 373 cm
Date: 1881/82
Artist: Koppala Subbarayudu of Irapalli
Provenance: Bandaru (Machilipatnam)
Captions: in Telugu

The majority of the incidents shown on this hanging are the same as those of cat. 12, but they appear in a different sequence. A Ganga *duppati* that appeared in the London salerooms in May 2011 displayed the same set of scenes, but yet again in a different order.² This suggests that the sequence of the narrative was dictated by the performers and that the painters followed their instructions. Collaboration between performers and painters is not uncommon; from anecdotal evidence, it appears that once the artists had finished their work, the storyteller would check it carefully for errors of placement of the scenes or figures and, if necessary, insist on amendments.³

As stated in the inscription above the Churning of the Ocean scene (fig. 23), the master dyer responsible for this work was Koppala Subbarayudu of Erapalle (Irapalli) who made this Ganga *duppati* in Bandaru in 1881/82.

The story is laid out on eight registers, of which only the eighth runs through the whole width of the cloth, whereas the remaining seven are accommodated around the central image of Gangamma (fig. 38). The narrative commences on the top right corner of the cloth with an image of Vinayaka.

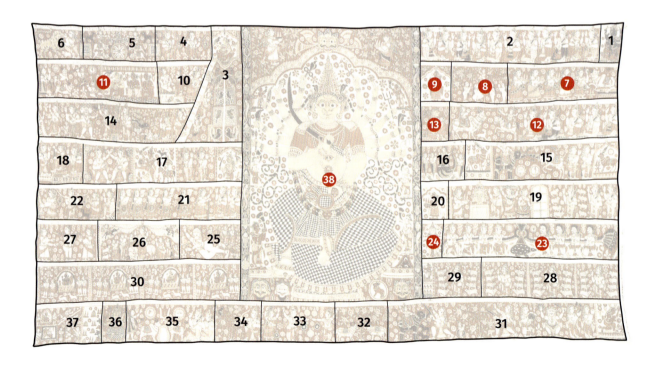

CAPTIONS

First register, to the right of the central tableau; from right to left:

1. *Sri Vinayaka.*

2. *Simhadriraju; Yeranukaraju; Nalanukkaraju; Pallikondaraju* [minister of Poluraju]; *Peddiraju; Amullu; Achutamullu; Ayataraju* [Aithamaraju?].

First register, to the left of the central tableau:

3. *Papanuka.*
   (see cat. 12.6)

4. *He* [Bhattiranna] *carries some food in a kavadi.*
   (see cat. 12.7)

5. *Katamaraju and Padmanaidu relax and play pachisi.* [Illegible] *have cows and bulls in Jannivada.*
   (see cat. 12.8)

6. *He has torn apart the tiger's mouth.*
   (see cat. 12.29; here the hero is identified as Kuppokondanna)

Second register, to the right of the central tableau; from right to left:

7. *Yeranuka Sita; Nalanuka Sita; Simhadri Sita and Sridevi worship with arati Pampadri Basavanna; Peddamma Devi burns camphor in the flame.* (fig. 7)

Fig. 7

This episode refers to events prior to the birth of Katamaraju. The locale is Pampadri, where Peddiraju and his brothers jointly ruled for seven years. Five women carrying trays with *arati* [camphor flame] and offerings approach the image of Pampadri Basavanna. Peddamma performs *puja*. The bull rejects her offering. **(see cat. 12.4)**

8. *Sri Krishnamurti climbs on the ponnachettu tree.* (fig. 8)

Krishna climbs on the *ponnachettu* tree on whose branches he has hung the clothes of the *gopis*. Strangely enough, the river, where the *gopis* are supposed to be bathing, is not shown. Krishna is rendered as a small boy with his hair tied in a topknot, naked but for his usual ornaments. **(see cat. 12.24)**

Fig. 8

Fig. 9

9. A woman offers *arati* to Gangamma. (fig. 9)

Second register, to the left of the central tableau:

10. Unidentified scene.

11. *Yerranappa [Yerrayya?] attacks Nellore fort with cows and bulls. Kundamadevi carries a parrot on her hand.* (fig. 11)

Fig. 11

This scene illustrates the beginning of the hostilities between Katamaraju and Siddhiraju, ruler of Nellore. The latter's wife, Kundamadevi, had a parrot whose chirping disturbed the grazing cows. One of Katamaraju's followers, Padma Raghava, shot an arrow at the bird, who flew back to his mistress, told her what happened, and died. The enraged Kundamadevi sent some Boyas to kill the herds of Katamaraju.

A thin vertical line with a chevron pattern separates this scene from the next: a Golla, clad in his blanket and carrying a curved stick, drives the cows in the fields. The animals are attacked by two Boyas armed with long spears. To the left and the right of the tableau are the Sun, seen frontally with a Vaishnava *namam* on his forehead, and the Moon, shown in profile with nose ring. This means that the events narrated here will never be forgotten as long as the Sun and the Moon will shine. **(see cat. 12.13)**

Third register, to the right of the central tableau; from right to left:

12. *Tikkanna mantri fights against Tamballa Brahmayya.* (fig. 12)

Siddhiraju sends a delegation to Katamaraju in order to settle the question of the grazing tax. The diplomatic mission fails, and he orders Tikkanna *mantri*, his commander-in-chief, to collect the tax from the Gollas. Tikkanna attacks the Gollas. Riding on a horse he fights against Tamballa who is mounted on a large bull. **(see cat. 12.15)**

Fig. 13 ← Fig. 12

13. *Yasodha breastfeeds Krishna.* (fig. 13)

(see cat. 12.16)

Third register, to the left of the central tableau:

14. *The heads of Valiketuvaraju were cut and carried by the eagle; Katamaraju fights against Valiketuvaraju; Peddamma Devi offers her bracelets* [illegible].

The eagle carries the severed heads of King Valiketuvaraju in its beak and flies towards a tree, beneath which lies Peddiraju. Katamaraju confronts the three-headed Valiketuvaraju. Behind Katamaraju are the goddess Gangamma and her brother, Poturaju.

Peddamma Devi, with her extended left hand, is engulfed by the flames. Near her stands a male figure (Bhattiranna?) flanked by a woman (Sridevi?) and by Katamaraju and his sister Papanuka. **(see cat. 12.31 and cat. 12.26)**

Fourth register, right of the central tableau, from right to left:

15. *Katamaraja and Padmanayudu worship the cow; Bolyavu fights.*

Katamaraju and Padmanayudu worship Bolyavu. Above it is the sun, and opposite it, two flames burn in a brazier. The animal, with a Vaishnava *namam* drawn on its hump, is sumptuously caparisoned. Its horn is covered by an elaborate metal sheath.

Bolyavu, with its long and sharp horn, attacks and stabs Nallasiddhi who is mounted on a black elephant and armed with a long spear. In the foreground, the Sun and the Moon are conspicuously shown, as in no. 11. The sequence ends with a depiction of Bolyavu standing before a brazier as described above. **(see cat. 12.17)**

16. *Sri Krishnamurti quells Kalinga.*

    (see cat. 12.20)

Fourth register, left of the central tableau:

17. *Karyavularaju pays homage to Hanuman; Kariyavularaju kicks Bethala* [commander-in-chief of Prataparudra of Orugallu, formerly Warangal]; *Karyavularaju fights against Bethala.*

    (see cat. 12.19)

18. *Puttamaraju* [son of Komaramma] *is shown a mirror.*

    The caption of this episode illustrated in cat. 12.28 speaks of a letter rather than of a mirror. The two drawings are very similar, and one wonders if there has been a lapse of the pen on the part of the scribe. **(see cat. 12.28)**

Fifth register on the right of the central tableau, from right to left:

19. *Simhadriraju, Peddiraju and Pallikonda Eddula* [minister of Poluraju], *share the bulls, the cows and the wealth; Komarakka carries the money-box.*

    The scene illustrated here refers to events prior to the birth of Katamaraju. Peddiraju and his brothers share their wealth before parting company. Komarakka carries the box containing the huge head of the goddess, Dana Ganga. It is eventually placed on a high pedestal and two women perform *puja* before it. **(see cat. 12.12)**

20. A female figure carries an *arati* tray with two lit camphor pellets and offers it to Gangamma, at the centre of the hanging.

Fifth register, on the left of the central tableau:

21. *Pallikonda Raju and Poluraju* [?] *are welcomed by the Jangalus and Silobhadevi* [illegible].

    (see cat. 12.18)

22. Unidentified episode.

    A female figure stands opposite a huge flame. A man, perhaps Bhattiranna, carrying a *kavadi* and flanked by a dog, seems to be the most relevant figure of this scene. A woman carrying a tray with two lit camphor pellets walks towards him. All four figures look towards the flame at the extreme left of the panel.

Sixth register, on the right of the central tableau; from right to left:

23. *Devatas and rakshasas churn the Milk Ocean; in the year Vrishaba [1881–82] in the month of Asoja [June/July], on the tenth day of the bright half of the month, on Monday at Bandaru [Machilipatnam], Koppala Subbarayudu, a resident of Erapalle has written this Ganga duppati.* (fig. 23)

Fig. 23

Four deities and four *rakshasas*, with hair standing on end, round eyes, moustache, side fangs and prominent teeth, churn the Milk Ocean. The *rakshasas* wear a *tripundra*-like *tilaka* on their forehead—a sign of their Shaiva affiliation. At the centre of the tableau is the tortoise which supports Mount Mandara, around which the five-headed snake, Vasuki, is coiled. Flanking Mount Mandara are the Sun and the Moon, depicted as already described in nos. 11 and 15. **(see cat. 12.36)**

24. *A Vaishnava dvarapala.* (fig. 24)

Sixth register, on the left of the central tableau:

25. *Sri Krishnamurti is tied to the mortar.*

26. *Sri Krishnamurti lifts Mount Govardhana.*
    (see cat. 12.40)

27. *Sri Krishnamurti plays the flute.*
    (see cat. 12.22)

Fig. 24

Seventh register, on the right of the central tableau; from right to left:

28. *Simhadriraju, Peddiraju and Pallikonda Eddula divide the bulls and the cows.*

    This is the continuation of the episode illustrated in no. 19—the division of the wealth and the herds among Peddiraju and his brothers. **(see cat. 12.10)**

29. *A devotee carries an arati tray, on which burn two camphor pellets, and offers it to Gangamma.*

    See nos. 9 and 20.

Seventh register, on the left of the central tableau:

30. *Nalanukaraju, Erranukaraju, Simhadriraju and Peddiraju divided the cattle and they travel in palanquins.*

This is the continuation of the episode illustrated in nos. 19 and 28. **(see cat. 12.2)**

Eighth register, from right to left:

31. *Viranayudu performs Shiva puja and takes the sword; Viranayudu plays and dances. Viranayudu cuts a tree; Viranayudu cuts the head of Siddhiraju's elephant.*
(see cat. 12.34)

32. *They tied the rams to trees.*

The caption does not specify who has tied the rams to the tree, whereas Mummaya and Pochayya are mentioned in the same episode illustrated in cat. 12.35. **(see cat. 12.35, centre)**

33. *Pochayya and Mummaya play tops; the top falls on the Komati's foot.*

Mummaya and Pochayya play tops. They have a whip in one hand, a top in the other, and three more tops are in the foreground. One of the tops hits the foot of the Komati girl—shown carrying a pot on the head and talking to the two youths.[4] **(see cat. no. 12.37)**

34. A male figure, perhaps Padma Raghava, a follower of Katamaraju, aims his arrows at a bird perched on the branches of a flowering tree and kills it.

This may be the depiction of the killing of Kundamadevi's pet parrot, which led to the subsequent destruction of the Golla herds by Nallasiddhi's troops. **(see cat. 12.9)**

35. *They call left and right their bulls and fill the trough with milk.*
(see cat. 12.11)

36. *Poluraju has sacrificed goats and given naivedyam to Aravali Gangamma.*
(see cat. 12.38)

37. *Peddiraju and Peddamma Devi go from Pampadri to Kalyani to beget children.* Written on the border in Latin script: -Ganga-

The caption does not mention either *chidi mari,* the hook-swinging scene, or Balarama, recognizable by his ploughshare, climbing on the pole. **(see cat. 12.38)**

38. Gangamma. (fig. 38)

Surrounded by two narrow vertical bands depicting the Paleru stream teeming with fish, tortoises and water snakes, the twelve-armed goddess Gangamma sits in *lalitasana* on a throne on whose basement are three 'masks'.[5] Of the two on the left: one has a Vaishnava *namam* on the forehead, the other a Shaiva *tripundra*; the one on the right displays a Vaishnava *namam*. Near it is the image of a diminutive cow

Ganga Duppati Machilipatnam

Fig. 38

inscribed in a white orb. To the right side of the throne is a mountain. The goddess is surrounded by six horn-players, who could be the Kommulavaru, who play and sing the *Katamaraju* ballads. The spandrels of the lobed arch above her head accommodate two winged female-figures bearing an *arati* tray. A particularly elaborate *kirttimukha* adorns the cusp of the arch. The goddess wears a sari with a black-and-white chequered pattern, and a red blouse; a garland of severed heads and one with a floral design adorn her waist. From her tall, elaborately wrought crown emerge two snakes and a flowering creeper whose curved tendrils, along with red rosettes, cover the background. Large *karnapattras* (leaf-shaped ornaments) are attached to the sides of her crown. She wears numerous jewellery items. On her forehead, above her mesmeric eyes, slightly reddened at the edges, a crescent-shaped *tilaka* is carefully drawn. **(see cat. 12.39)**

Notes

1. '*Duppati*' means blanket, see cat. 12, n. 2.
2. Bonham's Indian and Islamic Art Sale, 5 April 2011, Lot 379.
3. This was observed by Thangavelu while studying the painted scrolls from Telangana (Thangavelu 2011: 128).
4. See cat. 12, n. 10.
5. There is an uncanny resemblance between these masks and the 'demon masks' hanging today on the rear of trucks and at construction sites, etc.

Mahalakshmi Pithakam
MACHILIPATNAM

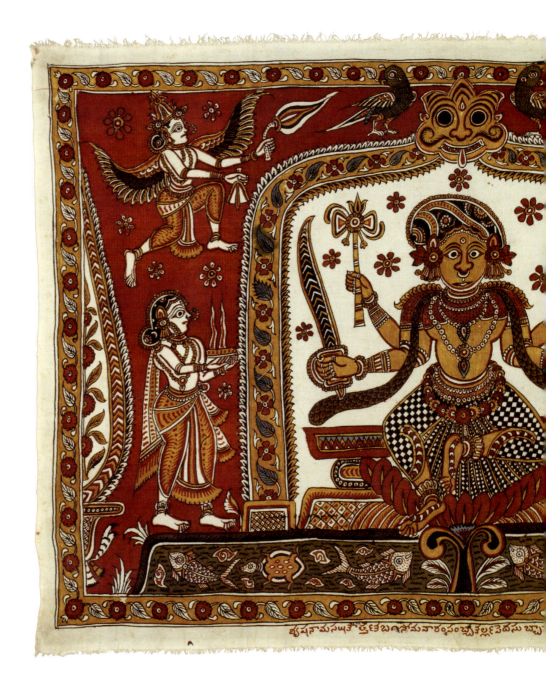

Mahalakshmi Pithakam Machilipatnam

14. Mahalakshmi *pithakam*
2104-1883 (IS)
Dimensions: 43 x 100.5 cm
Date: 1881–82 (Telugu cyclical year *Vrisha*)
Artist: Panchakalla Pedda Subbarayudu
Provenance: probably Machilipatnam
Caption: in Telugu

Mahalakshmi, 'the great Lakshmi', is one of the three major manifestations of Devi; her other two aspects being Mahakali and Mahasarasvati. These three manifestations are associated, respectively, with Vishnu, Shiva and Brahma. Mahalakshmi personifies the *rajas-guna* (i.e. the energy which promotes or upholds the activity of nature) of the great goddess and as such she is associated with both Vishnu and Shiva. This most powerful goddess is represented in many different ways and with a number of arms, which vary from four to eighteen.

CAPTION

1. *In the year Vrisha, on a Monday, Panchakalla Pedda Subbarayudu wrote this Mahalakshmi pithakam.*

   This Mahalakshmi *pithakam* (i.e. 'seat' of the goddess), prepared by Panchakalla Pedda Subbarayudu, the master dyer responsible for cat. 1 and cat. 12, was probably used for domestic rather than temple worship. Although the artist has signed and dated it, he has not mentioned where it was created. Its style is very similar to that of cat. 12.

   Set off by a white background enlivened by a small floral pattern, and surrounded by an arch culminating in a *kirttimukha*, the four-armed Mahalakshmi sits on a stepped *pitha*. Her feet rest on a lotus emerging from a lake. In her upper right hand, she carries a *damaru*; in her upper left a *trishula*; in her lower right hand is a sword, and in her lower left a *kapala*. A garland of flowers hangs around her neck. She wears a short red blouse and a lower garment with a check pattern, identical to that worn by Gangamma (see figs. 12.39, 13.38); a headgear similar to a *chayakkontai*, but bent to the right; and the usual ornaments. Flanking the arch, on a deep red background adorned by white flowers, are two flying *gandharvas* waving fly-whisks, and two ladies carrying *arati* trays. This tableau is defined on the left and the right by a typical Islamic motif widely used in the Machilipatnam *kalamkaris* made for the Iranian trade: two cypress-like shapes, emerging from vases.

Introduction to the Holy Sites

Four hangings depict these famous temple sites in Tamil Nadu: Srirangam, Tiruchendur, Tirupparankunram, and Alagar Koyil. While the first three display the temple complex and its surroundings, the last illustrates the *Chittirai* festival.

These cloths were made in the Madurai area. They are roughly of the same size, about 190 cm x 270 cm, and show similarities in style and layout, although there are considerable differences in their quality. Deities, places, and characters are identified by Tamil captions.

The central part of the cloth shows the access to the *garbha griha* (sanctuary) of the temple complex enshrining the main deity, the subsidiary shrines, and some of the most characteristic landscape features: e.g. the two branches of the Kaveri defining Srirangam island (cat. 17.1 and cat. 17.11), or the sea at Tiruchendur (fig. 15.8); the steep rocky hill with Sikandar Shah's *dargah* (fig. 16.16) at it summit, dominates the view of the Subrahmanya Temple at Tirupparankunram.

Vignettes disposed in four rows around the central tableau, illustrate either incidents connected with the site: e.g. the wedding of Subrahmanya and Devayanai at Tirupparankunram (fig. 16.2); or deities and holy personages at Srirangam. The temple *vahanas*, on which the deity is paraded on festival days, appear in cats. 15, 17 and 18.

The hanging devoted to the representation of the *Chittirai* festival of the Alagar Koyil (cat. 18) does not have a central tableau. The various scenes are laid out in four rows depicting different phases of the festival. Each row is separated from the foregoing by a narrow border enlivened by red dots. Occasionally white rosettes appear on the background of the vignettes.

The borders of the cloths depicting the Alagar Koyil temple festival and the Tiruchendur Temple and chariot festival display a very sober pattern constituted by elongated vase-shaped elements, and large eight-petalled flowers respectively. Those of the other two hangings are filled with lively scenes, such as, holy men and their disciples, devotees engaged in various penances at Tirupparankunram (fig. 16.7), and parked chariots and groves along the Kaveri at Srirangam (fig. 17.12).

The two sites illustrated in cat. 15 and cat. 16 are sacred to Murugan, the god also known by the Sanskrit names: Skanda, Subrahmanya and Karttikeya. Murugan's devotees recognize six holy sites linked to the career of their god;[1] of these, Tirupparankunram near Madurai and Tiruchendur on the Gulf of Mannar are the earliest historically linked to his cult.

Note

1. The remaining four are: Tiruttani in the north of Tamil Nadu, Palani in the west, Svamimalai at the centre. The identification of one site is unclear: Palamutircholai, near Alagar Koyil. The general consensus is that the deity is present on every hill.

Sri Subrahmanya Temple AT TIRUCHENDUR

The Subrahmanya Temple at Tiruchendur, some 51 kilometres east of Tirunelveli, is the second among the six places intimately connected to the career of the god. Sited on a small promontory extending into the Gulf of Mannar, this temple has a long history, dating back to the middle of the 9th century CE, according to epigraphic sources.[1] Apart from a few remains, nothing else dating from this early period has survived. The temple was substantially renewed at the turn of the 20th century and the shrine was re-consecrated in 1941.

Tiruchendur means 'village of the sacred battle'; according to tradition it is here that the young god conquered the proud *asura*, Surapadma. The local myth is a version of the story that can be found in both Sanskrit and Tamil literature.[2] The gods requested Subrahmanya to free them from the tyranny of Surapadma. Subrahmanya complied, and set up camp at Tiruchendur. Before engaging in the battle, he requested the divine architect, Maya, to build a Shiva temple near the sea so that he could worship the god before waging war on the *asura*. The battle against Surapadma and his hordes lasted five days; it was fought on land, in the air, and under water. On the sixth day, only Surapadma had survived and, despite his desperate situation, he decided to go on fighting. Indra then became Subrahmanya's *vahana*, the peacock. The battle continued four days longer, until the *vel*, Subrahmanya's spear, spotted Surapadma concealed at the bottom of the sea. At this point, the *asura* emerged as a huge mango tree and attacked the god. The *vel* then split the tree into two; Surapadma emerged in his real form and, yet again, was severed into two. One part of his body became Subrahmanya's peacock-*vahana*, thus relieving Indra of this charge, and the other became his rooster banner. Subrahmanya then returned to Tiruchendur and worshipped Shiva to atone for the killing of Surapadma.[3]

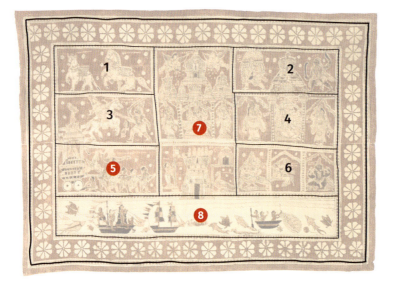

15. Sri Subrahmanya Temple, Tiruchendur

IM 31-1911

Dimensions: 190 x 271 cm
Date: 19th century
Provenance: Madurai area
Captions: in Tamil

Sri Subrahmanya Temple at Tiruchendur

CAPTIONS

1. *Bull-vahana and horse-vahana.*

2. *Ravanasura; Viran.*

    This is an unusual rendering of a famous incident in which Ravana was trapped beneath the massive Mount Kailasa. Here, the nine-headed king strides purposefully ahead, carrying on his head a pile of boulders symbolic of Mount Kailasa.[4] To the extreme right, Viran,[5] armed with an *aruval* (long, curved knife) and a dagger, strides ahead menacingly. The tiered superstructure of the Arumurugan Shrine (no. 4) spills into this scene, effectively separating Ravana from Viran.

3. *Virabahu[6] fights against Devasura.*

4. *Valli Amman, Arumurugan, Deivayanai Amman.*

    The sanctuary, capped by a tiered superstructure, culminates in a *stupika*, which protrudes into panel no. 2. The enshrined Arumurugan, i.e. six-headed Murugan, sits on a throne placed beneath a lobed arch. His twelve arms are devoid of attributes except for the lowermost left and right hands, carrying an imposing *vel*. Flanking Arumurugan's niche are those of his consorts: on his right is Valli Amman; on his left, Deivayanai.

5. *People pulling the chariot.[7]* (fig. 5)

Fig. 5

Murugan's processional image is two-armed and carries the *vel* in its hands. The chariot's superstructure, decorated with flags, consists of a *stupika* on which perches a peacock. A galloping winged horse is at the front of the chariot. Five men pull the conveyance by means of a thick rope, while a sixth removes the wedge from beneath its solid wooden wheels. A temple official, wearing a Maratha-style turban and a sash, emblazoned with a large badge across his chest, directs the whole operation.

6. *Subrahmanyasvami, Virabahudeva,[8] Vinayaka.*

7. [From top to bottom] *Gandharvas* [flanking the *gopura*] *Valli Amman, Sentiladipani, Deivayanai Amman.* [In the temple] *Battar* [priest], *gopuram, mayil madam.* (fig. 7)

    The temple, on the shore of the sea, is entered through an imposing *gopura* (entrance building) with a barrel-vaulted roof with *yali*-faces at either end, surmounted

Fig. 7

Fig. 8

by five *kalashas*. To the right and the left of the *gopura* are two small shrines capped by *stupikas*. The temple flagstaff is prominently shown to the left, and near it stands a Brahmin, in a dhoti, with his hair tied in a *kudumi* (knot). He carries a bell in his left hand and a lamp in his right. To the right is the *mayil matha* (peacock monastery) in which Subrahmaya's peacock is enshrined. The main shrine has an imposing superstructure, culminating in a dome flanked by two flying *gandharvas* who scatter flower petals on the enshrined deities. Beneath the central dome, Subrahmanya sits on a throne with the *vel* in his hands. He is flanked by his consorts, each in a separate shrine (see also, no. 4).

8. A seascape with boats sailing on a tranquil sea, whose waves are discreetly hinted in the background. (fig. 8)

The border is enlivened by large, eight-petalled lotuses.

Notes

1. L'Hernault 1978: 186.
2. E.g. the *Skanda Purana*, the epics, and Sangam poetry. Clothey 1972: 83.
3. Mementoes of the battle are to be seen near the temple: for instance, a fresh water spring near the sea indicates where the deity thrust his *vel* into the ground.
4. Ravana has ten heads, however, often in the South Indian renderings of this episode he is shown with only nine, as, according to a legend, while held captive under the mountain, he cut one of them and fashioned out of it a *vina*—which he carries in his central pair of hands—to accompany his hymns of praise to Shiva.
5. One of the nine warriors who accompany Subrahmanya in all his campaigns.
6. The first and foremost of among the nine warrior-companions of Subrahmanya.
7. Two twelve-day festivals (*brahmotsavas*) are celebrated at Tiruchendur: one in the month of *Masi* (February/March) and one in the month of *Avani* (August/September). On the tenth day, the three temple chariots are dragged through the ceremonial street, and on the eleventh, the float festival takes place.
8. See n.6.

Sri Subrahmanyasvami Temple
AT TIRUPPARANKUNRAM

Sri Subrahmanyasvami Temple at Tirupparankunram

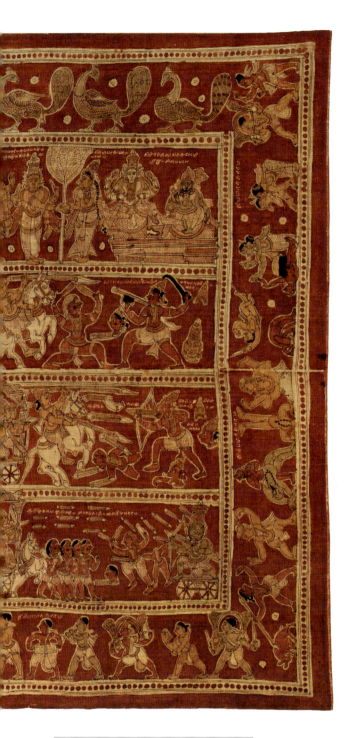

Tirupparankunram, a hill located about eight kilometres southwest of Madurai, is one of the most ancient holy places connected with the worship of Subrahmanya[1] (figs. 13–16). Here Murugan married Indra's daughter Deivayanai (or Devasena),[2] after he had proved himself by defeating Surapadma at Tiruchendur.[3] Atop this hill is the *dargah* (tomb) of 'Sekunder', i.e. the last ruler of the Madurai sultanate, Sultan Sikandar Shah (r. c. 1372–1377), whom Muslim pilgrims associate with Murugan.[4]

The hanging is divided into three vertical sections. The central one is occupied by a schematic view of the temple and the sacred hill, with its *tirthas* and the *dargah* on its summit. On the left are the battles between Subrahmanya and the *asuras* and a view of the temple tank; on the right, the wedding of Subrahmanya and Deivayanai in the presence of Indra, Minakshi and Chokkalingasvami (fig. 2), and further battles between the god and the *asuras*.

The numerous battle scenes indicate that either the artist or the patron was more interested in Subrahmanya's contests, rather than in his marriage. The borders illustrate, among others, the austerities performed by the pilgrims while circumambulating the sacred hill (fig. 17).

16. Sri Subrahmanyasvami Temple, Tirupparankunram
IM 29-1911
Dimension: 192 x 275.5 cm
Date: 19th century
Provenance: Madurai area
Captions: in Tamil

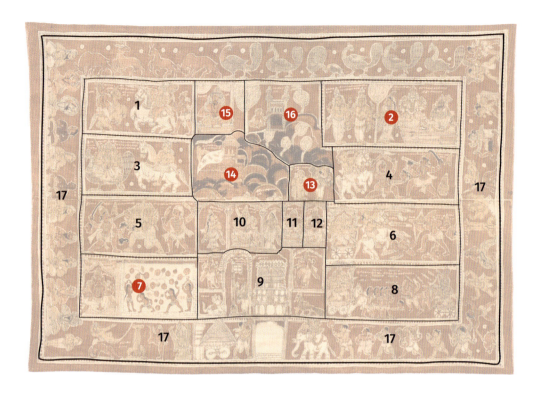

CAPTIONS

1. *Subrahmanyasvami and Virabahu[5] look for Surapadma.*

2. *Subrahmanyasvami marries Deivayanai; Deivayanai Ambal; Chokkalingasvami; Minakshi Ambal.* (fig. 2)

Fig. 2

On the left, Indra, recognizable by the *vajra* in his right upper hand, blesses the marriage of his daughter Deivayanai with Subrahmanya. The couple stands opposite a tree, Subrahmanya carries *tanka*s in his upper hands, and his lower right reaches

Sri Subrahmanyasvami Temple at Tirupparankunram

for Deivayanai's right hand. To the right are the tutelary deities of nearby Madurai, Minakshi and Chokkalingasvami.

3. *Suran* [Surapadma] *has taken the form of a peacock and Subrahmanyasvami sits on it.*[6]

4. *Virabahu fights against Surapadma.*

5. *The end of the battle between Subrahmanyasvami and Surapadma.*

6. *Battle between Lord Arumurugan* [i.e. six-headed Murugan] *and Gajamukhasura* [elephant-faced *asura*].

7. *Vighnesvara, Sravana Poikai.* (fig. 7)

Fig. 7

Near the temple is the Sravana Lake, filled with lotus flowers, and with steps on three sides. In its water, four pilgrims are engaged in their ablutions. At a short distance is a small Vighneshvara shrine.

8. *Battle between Arumurugan and Simhamukhasura* [lion-faced *asura*].

9–12. The temple

Labels: *Vrishaba mandapa, kodimaram* [flagstaff] *and Battar; gopura, mayil mandapa;* [above the bull's image and above the peacock *mandapa*:] *dvarapala.*

Flanking the entrance *gopura* are two buildings enshrining the *dvarapalas*.

The shrines

Labels: *Deivayanai Amman, Subrahmanyasvami, Valli Amman, Durgai Amman, Vighnesvara.*

[From left to right] Deivayanai Amman, her consort Subrahmanyasvami seated on a throne, and on his left is his second consort, Valli Amman (no. 10).

The remaining two shrines on the right are dedicated to Durgai Amman (no. 11) and Vighnesvara (no. 12). Durgai Amman's hair surrounds her face like a halo of flames.

She has eight arms and carries in one of her right hands the *trishula*, prongs downwards. Next to her sits Vighnesvara.

13–16. The mountain (figs. 13–16)

Labels: [On the mountain] *Tirupparankunram mountain*; *Dandayudhapani*. *Kasivisvanatha, Svaminathasvami*; *sannyasi*; [above the *dargah* on the mountain top] *pallivasal*.

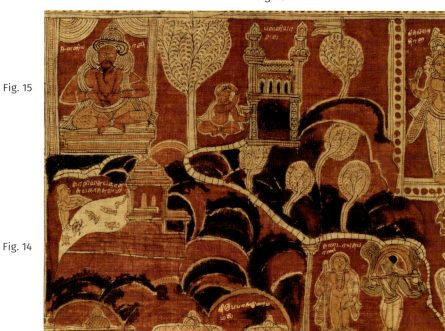

Fig. 16

Fig. 15

Fig. 14

Fig. 13

Behind the five shrines soars the mountain with its boulders and groves. On the right are the steps that lead to its summit; the shrines which pilgrims visit on their way up the hill are clearly shown. The first is a small temple dedicated to Dandayudhapani, the form of Subrahmanya worshipped at Palani (no. 13), and near it is a pilgrim bearing a *kavadi* on his shoulder. The next temple, dedicated to Kasivisvanathasvami, enshrines two *lingas* (no. 14). A pilgrim bathes in a small tank nearby. Proceeding along the steps, another shrine shelters a *sannyasi* (no. 15). Finally, at the top of the mountain is the mosque, with a Muslim pilgrim who has come to worship at the *dargah* of Sikandar.

Borders

Top border: Peacocks, a deer and three does.

The solid russet background is enlivened by small rosettes.

Left border: *Circumambulation of the mountain.*

A row of yogis, dressed in dhotis, wearing ornaments of *rudraksha* beads. At the end of the row stands a disciple with flowing hair, with his hands in *anjali mudra*.

Sri Subrahmanyasvami Temple at Tirupparankunram

Right border: *Circumambulation of the mountain.*

Pilgrims walk around the mountain, engaging in various penances.

Bottom border: *Circumambulation of the mountain.*

At the centre is the entrance to the temple and a building near which is parked the chariot, covered by a thatched roof. A temple attendant carrying an umbrella waits for a procession coming from the right to reach the temple entrance: a caparisoned elephant carrying a person with a *kalasha*, in whose mouth is stuck a coconut, is followed by a standard-bearer, two musicians and two pilgrims bearing *kavadis* on their shoulders and sticks in their hands. Between them is a Brahmin holding a palm-leaf book (fig. 17). To the left of the chariot are further five persons engaging in yogic exercises and various forms of penance.

Fig. 17   Bottom border

Notes

1. This is testified by a relief of Shiva, Uma and Skanda, cut in the rock near the top of the hill in 773 CE, under the patronage of the Early Pandyas.
2. This mythical marriage is commemorated in the most important festival of the year, the *Pankuni Uttiram*, held in late March when the alignment of the Sun, stars and planets are particularly auspicious for weddings.
3. See cat. 15.
4. Branfoot 2003: 147–179.
5. The first and foremost of Murugan's companions.
6. See cat. 15 for details on Surapadma.

Sri Ranganathasvami Temple
AT SRIRANGAM

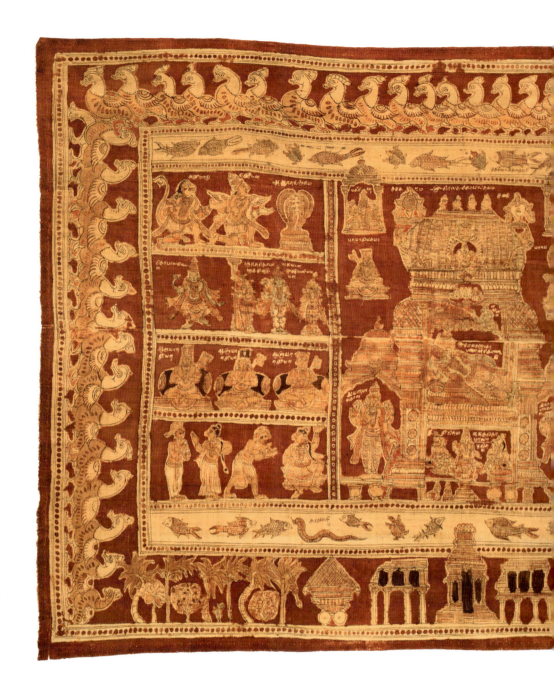

Sri Ranganathasvami Temple at Srirangam

The Sri Ranganathasvami Temple on Srirangam island in the Kaveri River has a long history, reputedly reaching back to the early centuries CE.[1] The core of the present complex, however, was founded probably during the Chola period (9th–13th cent. CE), and received its first substantial additions under the patronage of the Pandya and Hoysala dynasties. Under the Vijayanagara and Nayaka rulers in the 16th and 17th centuries, it was systematically enlarged and grew into a town consisting of seven concentric enclosures built around the main sanctuary. The latest important addition to the complex was the southern entrance *gopura*, 72 metres high, which was completed in 1987.

By depicting the two branches of the Kaveri River at the top and the bottom of the cloth (nos. 1 and 11), the artist clearly conveys the location of temple. The focus of the composition is the central sanctuary enshrining the reclining Sri Ranganatha (fig. 10).

The most important shrines of the innermost enclosures are shown behind the main sanctuary. Vignettes to the left and right of the central tableau illustrate some of the temple *vahanas* on which the deity is paraded through the streets of the town during the festivals (nos. 2, 3); important images worshipped in various shrines in the complex (nos. 4, 5); the *alvars*, poet-saints (7th–9th cent. CE), whose compositions play a major role in the liturgy (nos. 6, 7); and finally, scenes of music and dance (nos. 9, 10). Particularly interesting is the depiction of chariots and groves on the lower border of the cloth (fig. 12).

17. Sri Ranganathasvami Temple, Srirangam
IM 30-1911
Dimensions: 197 x 273 cm
Date: 19th century
Provenance: Madurai area
Captions: in Tamil

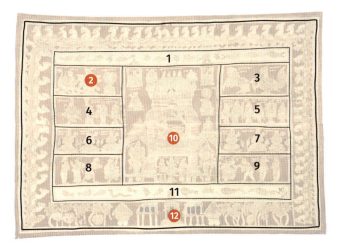

171

Labels:

1. *Kollidam–Kaveri*

    The hanging's top and bottom registers show the two branches of the Kaveri defining the island of Srirangam.

2. *Hanuman, Garuda, the many-headed snake Ananta.* (fig. 2)

    Fig. 2

    The top register is occupied by some of the temple *vahanas* used during the various temple festivals, in particular during the yearly *brahmotsava*.

3. *Horse-vahana; hamsa-vahana.*

4. *Gopalakrishna, Nandagopalakrishna* [both, aspects of Krishna]; *Nachchiyar* ['consort'], *Rukmini*.

5. *Kodandapani* [Rama], *Nachchiyar* [i.e. Sita]; *Rukmini; Garudalvar* [Garuda], *Mannarusvami* [Rajagopalasvami], *Nachchiyar Amman* ['lady consort'].

6. *Alvars.*

7. *Alvars.*

8. Scene of music and dance.

9. *Dancer, maddale* [drum] *player, tala* [cymbal] *player, trumpeter.*

10. [On the superstructure] *chakra; gopura; shankha.*

    [Flanking the shrine] *dvarapalakas;* [in the shrine] *Shri Balakanayakar reclining and Vibhishana.*

    [Opposite the main deity] *Shridevi, Nandagopala, Bhudevi.*

    [To the left of the temple; (illegible) in the temple] *Mahadeva* [?].

    [To the right of the temple; (illegible) in the temple] *Mahalakshmi.*

    (fig. 10)

    The central tableau depicts the innermost shrine at the heart of the Sri Ranganatha Temple complex. The sanctuary is capped by a superstructure culminating in a barrel-vaulted roof, surmounted by four *kalashas*, and adorned, at the corners, by the Vaishnava emblems, *chakra* and *shankha*, and beneath them *yali*-heads protrude from the roof. At its centre, a niche enshrines the image of Paravasudeva. Beneath it, on the sanctuary's door lintel, are *shankha, namam* and *chakra*. In its interior, the two-armed Balanayakar (i.e. Ranganatha) reclines on the coils of the serpent Ananta, whose extended hoods form a canopy above his head. A diminutive Vibhishana flies above the reclining god.

Opposite the reclining image are the *utsva beras* (festival images): the two-armed Nandagopala, flanked by his seated consorts, Sridevi and Bhudevi. Some ritual implements and two vessels are arranged opposite the images. The main shrine is guarded to the left and to the right by two four-armed *dvarapalas*. At their feet are further three ritual vessels[2] and a *shatari*, the crown on which the feet of Vishnu are embossed.

Few of the subsidiary shrines in the innermost *prakara* (enclosure) of the temple are depicted here; in the top left corner is a small temple enshrining a four-armed Vaishnava image. In the top right corner, in a similar building, the enshrined image is identified as Mahalakshmi. Two further figures, the one to the left, of Ramanuja seated, and the one to the right, of yet another *acharya* (teacher), seated, his head sheltered by the heads of Ananta, complete the tableau.

Fig. 10

11. *Kaveri*.

Borders

Borders with *hamsa* motifs are on the top, left and right sides of the cloth.

The lower border is of particular interest, because it is one of the very few examples of landscape painting in Indian art (fig. 12). At its centre is marked a rather simplified *gopura*-like structure. Flanking it are two tower-like buildings with exterior staircases: these are used by the priests to place the processional images onto the chariots. Two chariots are parked nearby; their massive chassis, with solid wooden wheels, are covered by a temporary roof of palm-leaf screens. At either side, groves with coconut palms, plantains trees and shrubs suggest the lush landscape surrounding the temple.

Fig. 12   *Lower border*

Notes

1. Among Vaishnavas this temple is simply known as '*koyil*' i.e. 'the temple'. It is the first among the 108 sacred Vaishnava *divyadeshams* (divine abodes). Srirangam was the residence, among others, of Ramanuja (d. 1137 CE), the founder of the Sri Vaishnava community. This temple is the centre of the southern tradition (*tengalai*) of Sri Vaishnavism.

2. For an explanation of the symbolism of the five vessels placed in the innermost sanctuary of the temple, see Hari Rao 1967: 129.

Alagar Koyil
CHITTIRAI FESTIVAL

This hanging depicts the *Chittirai* festival, the most important yearly event at the temple of Sundararaja Perumal (a form of Vishnu), at Alagar Koyil, some 20 kilometres north-east of Madurai.[1] Locally the deity is known as Alagar, or Kallalagar, 'the beautiful Lord of the Kallars', a warrior community inhabiting that area which was, according to the local tradition, conquered by Alagar, and became his bodyguards.[2]

Besides Alagar the second most-revered deity is Karuppannasvami or Karuppusvami, the 'Black Lord', the family deity of the Kallars. As the name says, he is dark-skinned, accepts animal sacrifices, and has a fierce temperament. Generally, he is shown striding purposefully ahead, brandishing the *aruval*, a sharp machete-like knife, and carrying a mace (fig. 16).[3]

The Alagar Koyil festival takes place in the month of *Chittirai* (April/May). The first four days of this event overlap the last four of the great *Chittirai* festival of Madurai. In the past, the festivals were unconnected and took place at different times. Eventually Tirumala Nayaka joined them together for both political and devotional reasons.[4]

According to the tradition, Alagar is believed to be the brother of Goddess Minakshi, the patron deity of Madurai, and as such he is invited to participate in her wedding which takes place there. The exact time of the wedding is not made clear to him, so that when after some days of travel he and his entourage reach the Vaigai River, he meets Kudalalagar (another aspect of Vishnu worshipped in Madurai) who tells him that the wedding has already taken place. Alagar, insulted that the ceremony has been celebrated without him, gives the presents for the bride to Kudalalagar, but refuses to enter the city. He then turns around, and proceeds along the north bank of the Vaigai, stops in Vandiyur for the night and returns to the Alagar Hills on the next day.

The deity, Alagar, is on his way for a total of six days, accompanied by his entourage, by Karuppannasvami and his devotees. Magnificently dressed and decorated, the deity, accompanied by a huge procession, proceeds from Alagar Koyil towards Madurai on various conveyances, such as a palanquin (no. 14), an elephant, a golden horse (no. 11), and the Garuda (no. 12) and Shesha *vahanas*.

Among Karuppannasvami's followers are some who undergo extreme penances, others who dance and are eventually possessed by the deity (nos. 17, 18). The relevance of the Kallars in this festival is evident by the amount of time the procession spends at various sites either owned or sponsored by them.

18. Alagar Koyil *Chittirai* festival
IM 27-1911
Dimensions: 185.7 x 262.8 cm
Date: 19th century
Provenance: Madurai area
Captions: in Tamil

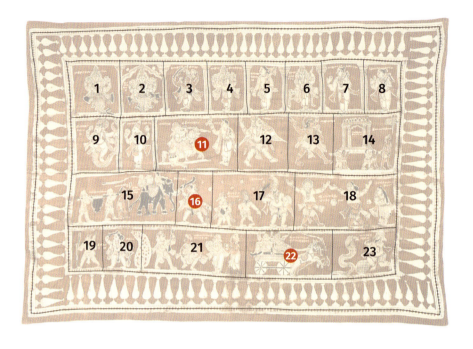

Labels:

First register

> This, and part of the second register depict the enactment of the ten *avataras*, which takes place on the evening of the sixth day, when the deity is on his way back to Alagar Koyil.[5]

Divided into eight panels, the first register depicts eight of the ten *avataras*:

1. *Macchavataram.*

2. *Kurmavataram.*

3. *Varahavataram.*

> Although the head is clearly that of a boar, the sword in his upper right hand and the shield in the lower left, suggest that this is Kalki, the future incarnation of Vishnu, rather than Varaha (see no. 10).

4. *Narasimhavataram.*

5. *Vamanavataram.*

6. *Ramavataram.*

7. *Parashuramavataram.*

8. *Balaramavataram.*

Second register

9. *Buddhavataram.*

   Krishna as Kalingamardana, is identified as Buddha *avatara* in the caption.

10. *Kalikavataram.*

    Despite the horse head, which points to Kalki, this is Varaha. Instead of carrying sword and shield in two of his hands, this image has *chakra* and *shankha* in its upper hands and the lower ones are in *abhaya* and *varada mudras* (see no. 3).

Chittirai festival procession

11. *Alagarsvami coming on the horse*; *Battar.* (fig. 11)

    The processional image of Alagarsvami mounted on his *vahana*, the horse. Opposite the *utsava murti* (festival image) stands a *pujari* with his hair tied in a topknot, carrying a bell in his left hand and a *dipa vriksha* (tree-shaped oil lamp) in his right.

12. and 13. *Garudalvar; Hanuman.*

14. *Palanquin; umbrella bearer.*

Fig. 11

Third register

15. *Undiyal box* [offering container]; *person holding fire-crackers; riders on an elephant.*

16. *Karuppusvami* (fig. 16)

    Karuppusvami, the guardian of the Kallalagar temple, strides ahead. His menacing stance, brandishing the *aruval* in his raised right arm, his powerful mace in his left, and his bushy moustache, reveal his awesome character.

17. *Bagpipe player; clown.*

    A man holds what looks like a bagpipe; however, this is probably a goat-skin bag full of turmeric water, which he squirts on the onlookers. Clowns are among the followers of the deity. The presence of these characters is one of the features of Alagar's procession along the riverbed.

18. *Possessed dancers; audience.*

    Two men dance beneath two large dummies which they carry over their heads and shoulders. The dummies depict a wild-haired man with large eyes and wide open arms, and his large-eyed, bare-breasted wife. This scene, according to the label, shows 'possessed dancers' performing for the benefit of a woman—described as 'audience' in the caption—who gazes at them in awe, with her hands folded in *anjali mudra*.[6]

Fig. 16

Fourth register

19. and 20. *Tiri...* [unclear], *Karuppusvami.*

A turbaned man, perhaps a 'coil bearer' (*tiriyattakkarar*), carries a long rod in the right, and a coil of tightly packed cloth in the left. The rod is used to beat oneself at regular intervals throughout Alagar's journey; the cloth, soaked in oil to make it smoulder, is held close to the body.[7] Behind him is Karuppusvami armed with *aruval* and mace.

21. *Musicians.*

22. *English people in a chariot.* (fig. 22)

Two foreigners in long trousers, jackets, shoes and, rather incongruously, in turbans, ride on a chariot drawn by horses.

23. *Snake charmer.*

Fig. 22

Borders

The borders display a pattern constituted by elongated vase-shaped elements, as in cat. 11.

Notes

1. Although the core of the temple dates to the 12th-century Pandya period, it was substantially enlarged and refurbished under Tirumala Nayaka of Madurai (r. 1623–1659).

2. The story of how Alagar defeated the Kallars, and how they became his most devoted and faithful servants, is related in Hudson 1982: 125. The connection of the Kallars with the Alagar temple and possibly with the journey festival dates from at least the 17th century (Hudson 1982: 137).

3. There is no iconic representation of him at Alagar Koyil. His shrine is the actual eastern *gopura* of the temple, or, to be more precise, its doors. Thus his role as guard of the temple parallels the traditional role played by the Kallars for the ruler of Madurai and for the neighbouring villages.

4. Hudson 1982: 137–38.

5. Possibly this series alludes to the all-night representation of the *avataras*, one of the most auspicious events for the devotees, which takes place on the full moon night in a small village near Madurai (Hudson 1982: 107).

6. In an e-mail of 20 May 2008, Indira V. Peterson refers to an important Tamil novel of the 1950s: *Tillana Mohanambal* by Kalaimani (Kothamangalam Subbu) in which the author describes the Alagar Koyil festival at the beginning of the 20th century: "... The dance image surely refers to a type of dummy dance called 'Puuta AaTTam' (Tamil 'puutam' in the sense of 'bhuta', a demon, spirit, ghost, monster, etc.). ...."

7. The 'coil bearers' were those who "became possessed by Karuppannacami, who then told the devotees of their faults, how they could be corrected, and what would be the fruits of their devotion." (Hudson 1982: 128)

The Life of Christ SRIKALAHASTI

This hanging is the work of Jonnalagadda Gurappa Chetty, one of the most renowned exponents of the art of *kalamkari*. He lives and works in Srikalahasti where, at the age of 13, he started learning the art of *kalamkari* from his father. "…His works have been exhibited in several foreign locations including Vienna, UK, Australia, China, and Canada. He was honoured with the title of 'Shilpa Guru' in 2002 by the Crafts Council of India. He won the Presidential National Award for Crafstmanship in 1976, Kamaladevi Vishwa Karigar Award and Tulasi Samman from Bharat Kala Bhavan, Bhopal."[1] Gurappa Chetty was honoured with the Padma Shri in 2008.

In this remarkable work, the artist explores a subject completely removed from the Hindu tradition. In so doing, he created a fascinating work displaying an admirable synthesis of traditional Indian and Western imagery. The illustrated episodes are drawn mainly from the Gospel according to Luke, although some are drawn from John (nos. 24, 25, 32, 33, 35) and Matthew (no. 29).

The work is laid out in nine rows around the central scene, strongly reminiscent of the classic *Ramapattabhisheka*: Christ surrounded by disciples and devotees (fig. 39). With its vivid palette, scenes filled with figures, landscape elements, and the traditional decorations enlivening the upper borders, this hanging is, at first sight, totally removed from relative simplicity of the 19th-century stylistic idiom, e.g. cat. 3. A *horror vacui* compels the artist to fill every available space with decorations. The display of virtuosity is breathtaking, but at times it distracts from the important elements of a given scene.

A careful look at the details, however, reveals how deeply this work is indebted to the Srikalahasti tradition. For example: the figures in profile, the limited repertoire of *mudras,* the details of costumes such as billowing scarves and the great variety of textile patterns. The first scene of the hanging depicts Ganesha surrounded by devotees, as usual in the Srikalahasti *kalamkari* tradition (fig. 1). It is followed by an intriguing rendering of a *yogi* seated on a lotus, beneath a tree. Although the text identifies this figure as 'the artist', it is probably meant to be the evangelist, who by divine inspiration—visualized as the ray of light originating from a star—writes the life of Jesus.

The artist experiments with some new features such as renderings of nature: stars (nos. 2 and 10); multicoloured clouds around flying angels (no. 7); or stormy ones as in the remarkable scene of the tempest on the sea (fig. 29). The sea (nos. 22, 23), with the placidly bobbing crafts, or agitated by the winds and

19. The Life of Christ
IS 1-1983
Dimensions: 218 x 306 cm
Date: 1981
Artist: Jonnalagadda Gurappa Chetty
Provenance: Srikalahasti
Captions: in Telugu

under a pelting rain (no. 29). His trees with gnarled trunks have lush crowns filled with a profusion of colourful blooms (no. 7). Cityscapes, inspired by Western art, figure prominently in the background of a number of scenes (e.g. fig. 4). There is yet another departure from the traditional iconography. In the 19th-century works, the *en face* view was the sole prerogative of the main character and exclusively in the central tableau of the hanging (e.g. Rama). Here, however, Jesus, whose head is consistently shown with a halo, appears *en face*, not only in the central scene, but also in nos. 23, 32, 38. Furthermore, in nos. 10, 14 and 15, some figures are visible from the waist up: this trait is a stylistic innovation, not found in 19th-century *kalamkaris*.

The artist takes great pleasure in diversifying the characters of each scene by giving them different hues: green, white, beige, red, and different attires. Especially intriguing are the varieties of headgears displayed in this work: crowns, turbans, head cloths—e.g. a veil covers Mary's head, surrounded by a halo; this iconographic detail is consistently observed throughout. Some characters are in traditional Indian costumes: the angels with multicoloured wings are dressed in dhoti and *angavastra*, wear crowns and the usual jewellery. Zacharias is depicted as a Brahmin, with a conspicuous *kudumi* tied at the back of his head, and wears a *yajnopavita* hanging from his left shoulder and ornaments of *rudraksha* beads (fig. 4).

Herod, proudly seated on his throne brandishing a sword and sporting a moustache, looks like the 'baddies' of Indian cinema (no. 9). The same iconographic type is used for Pilate (no. 36). Fly-whisk bearers and guards are dressed in a peculiar Indo-Roman costume: a leather strip skirt above a dhoti and a feathery headgear (e.g. fig. 37). The representation of Satan is a mixture of the traditional *rakshasa*-iconography and that of the goddess Kali: his short lower garment strongly reminiscent of the skirt of severed arms worn by Kali (fig. 21). The episode of the wedding at Canaan (no. 24) is depicted in the traditional manner: the couple flank the sacred tree, opposite which the sacrificial flame is kindled by a Brahmin. The chariot on which the three kings travel (no. 10) is inspired by those in Indian mythological films, as well as in the *Amar Chitra Katha* comics. Yet another trait borrowed from the comics is seen in no. 26, in which the ailing youth is seen in a cloud above the centurion's[2] head.

The entrance to the prison in which St John is held captive is adorned by a number of mouldings, among which some display floral motifs, and some are shaped like lotus petals—similarly to the plinths of Indian sacred buildings (no. 17).

The only slip of the pen observed in the inscription is in no. 33: *Martha is drying Jesus's feet with her hair.* It should read: Mary Magdalene.

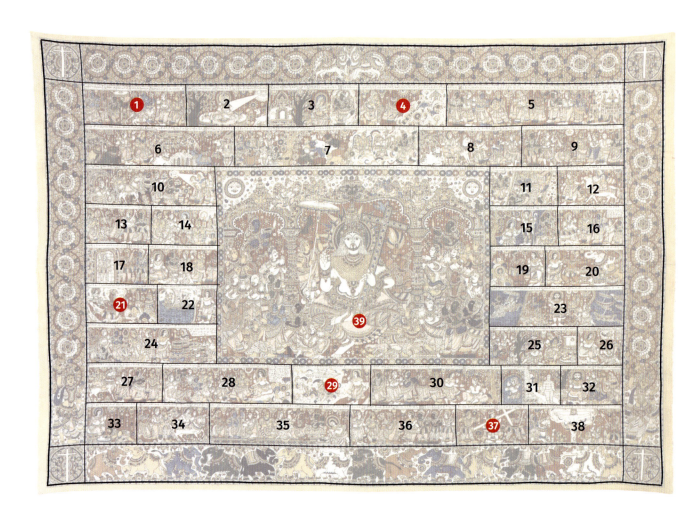

CAPTIONS

First register

1. *Before commencing to write the life of Jesus Christ, the artist pays homage to Ganesha.* (fig. 1)

Fig. 1

2. *By the grace of God, the artist starts to write the story of Jesus Christ.*

3. *The archangel Gabriel tells Mary that Jesus Christ will be born unto her.*

4. *Mary goes to the city of Judaea where she meets Zacharias and his wife Elisabeth. She [Mary] embraces her.* (fig. 4)

Fig. 4

Zacharias, depicted as a Brahmin, is at the centre of the scene. To his right, Mary embraces Elisabeth. The right portion of the scene shows a hilly tract with a long road winding among boulders and trees, leading to a distant settlement.

5. *Zacharias and Elisabeth had a son, he was named John. Zacharias was the priest on the hill. The guests are blessing the baby.*

Second register

6. *In the manger, in Bethlehem, Jesus Christ was born from the sacred womb of Mary.*

7. *It was very cold, the shepherd had lit a fire. They saw the angels coming down [from heaven] announcing that Jesus Christ was born in the manger, and then they disappeared.*

8. *The shepherds brought their best goats as a gift to the infant Jesus.*

9. *The Kings from the East saw the star, followed it, and arrived to King Herod.*

Third register

10. *The Kings from the East followed the star and brought royal gifts to the infant Jesus.*

11. *The angels appeared in their dreams and told them to flee from King Herod.*

12. *Following the angels' advice, Joseph and Mary took Christ to Egypt.*

Fourth register

13. *King Herod sends the servants to look for two-year-old children.*

14. *Jesus Christ participates in a discussion with the learned men in the temple.*

15. *On the banks of the Marda River* [Nahr al-Urdun, i.e. Jordan], *John baptized Jesus.*

16. *The people living in the hills come and ask John to baptize them also.* [In the insert in the panel] *He says, "You should do your duties properly".*

Fifth register

17. *John is imprisoned in the dungeon.*

18. *Jesus Christ teaches the important duties of Christianity.*

19. *Satan comes, shows some pieces of rock to Jesus, and asks him to transform them into bread.*

20. *To test him, Satan tempts him with masses of wealth.*

Sixth register

21. *Satan takes Jesus on top of a hill and asks him to jump.* (fig. 21)

Fig. 21

Satan, in flying posture, similar to the traditional renderings of the flying Hanuman, carries, seated on his right hand, a diminutive, impassive Jesus. They fly through the sky and land atop of a mountain on which are two buildings reminiscent of Western renderings of the Far Eastern pagodas.

Satan's lower garment is strongly reminiscent of the skirt of severed arms worn by Kali, and adorned by a girdle from which hang skulls. Around his neck he wears a necklace with a skull pendant. Horns grow out of his head on which he wears the feathery headgear. His half-open mouth reveals a set of crooked teeth, and his eyes are round.

22. *The fishermen sailed off to catch fish, but were disappointed. Jesus Christ blessed them.*

The fishermen wear an elaborate version of the simple pointed caps, made of palm leaves, typical of Odisha and Coastal Andhra.

23. *The fishermen Simon and Peter thus blessed by Jesus caught plenty of fish and became his disciples.*

Seventh register

24. *In Galilee, Jesus was attending a wedding with his mother. There was not enough drink for the guests and she was worried. Then Jesus Christ, by his miraculous powers, transformed six barrels of water into drink [wine] and she was comforted.*

25. *The Samaritan woman gave him water to quench his thirst and his disciples were surprised.*

26. *A powerful person asks Jesus Christ to save his child who was ill.*

Eighth register

27. *While he* [the 'powerful person'] *was returning, some people told him that his son had recovered.*

28. *Many came to hear the teaching of Jesus. He arranged food for them by giving them one fish and five loaves. By his miraculous powers they were all fed. And Andrew served them.*

29. *The disciples were caught in a storm and were saved by Jesus Christ.* (fig. 29)

Under a pelting rain, five of Jesus's disciples are caught in a storm at sea. Their craft is tossed by high waves. Jesus, unperturbed, watches the scene from the shore. Particularly effective is the juxtaposition of the dramatic events shown on the left side of the scene: the sinking craft with its sail in tatters, the torrential rain and the high seas; and on the right, the calm surrounding the figure of Jesus.

Fig. 29

30. *Jesus Christ restored the sight of a blind man and showed him the earth in front of him.*

31. *The blind man took a dip in the pond and got his sight back.*

32. *Lazarus died, was buried, and Jesus resuscitated him. Thus Martha and the others greatly rejoiced.*

Ninth register

33. *Martha* [Mary Magdalene] *is drying Jesus's feet with her hair.*

34. *Jesus Christ rides on a donkey, followed by Lazarus and others.*

35. *Jesus Christ washes the feet of Simon, Peter and others, to make them clean.*

36. *Pilate passes judgment on Jesus, declaring him a criminal, and orders his soldiers to nail him to the cross.*

37. *Jesus Christ carries the cross to Mount Calvary.* (fig. 37)

    Fig. 37

    Jesus, tired and emaciated, followed by a guard armed with a whip and a spear, drags the cross on the way to the Calvary.

38. *There he was nailed to the cross. Mary and his disciples looked at him and were disconsolate.*

39. *After Jesus Christ had been crucified, and died, on the third day he won death, came back to life and gave darshana to the disciples* [appeared before his disciples], *who paid homage to him.* (fig. 39)

    Fig. 39

    Jesus sits in *lalitasana* pose on a throne; a sun-like halo surrounds his head. In his left hand he carries the cross, and his right hand is in teaching attitude. He is flanked by a parasol and a fly-whisk bearer, and by his disciples and other persons. In the foreground, a woman, possibly Mary Magdalene, prostrates at his feet, and to his left is Mary, with her hand in *anjali mudra*. The scene is set in a three-bayed hall with cusped arches surmounted by *kirttimukhas*. In the outer bays, along with Jesus's disciples, are lamp bearers. In the left and right corners of the central tableau are respectively the sun and the moon as well as *gandharvas* carrying flower garlands, blowing their trumpets and strewing flower petals on the scene.

Borders

Of particular interest are the borders of this *kalamkari*. At the four corners of the cloth is a cross, inscribed in a circle. On either of the vertical sides of the cloth, a *latasundari* clutches a lush creeper that terminates at the centre of the top border. The end of the creeper merges with two depictions of Kamadhenu, facing one another. The lower border is enlivened by an elephant motif.

Notes

1. *The Hindu*, 26 January 2008.
2. Described in the caption as a 'powerful person'.

Bibliography

Archer, M., *Company Paintings: Indian Paintings of the British Period*, Victoria and Albert Museum/Mapin, London/Ahmedabad 1992

Arni, S. and Chitrakar, M., *Sita's Ramayana*, Tara Books, Chennai 2011

Barnes, R., Cohen, S., Crill, R., *Trade, Temple & Court: Indian Textiles from the Tapi Collection*, India Book House, Mumbai 2002

Bernier, F., *Travels in the Mogul Empire A.D. 1656–1668*, revised edition by Archibald Constable, Westminster 1891

Bhagavata Purana, translated and annotated by G.V. Tagare, Ancient Indian Tradition and Mythology, vols 7–11, Motilal Banarasidass, Delhi 1978

Birdwood, G.C.M., *The Industrial Arts of India*, Chapman & Hall, London 1880

Blackburn, S., *Inside the Drama House: Rama Stories and Shadow Puppet Plays in South India*, University of California Press, Los Angeles/Berkeley/London 1996

Bose, M. (ed.), *The Ramayana Revisited*, Oxford University Press, New York 2004

Branfoot, C., 'The Madurai Nayakas and the Skanda Temple at Tirupparankundram', in *Ars Orientalis* vol. 33 (2003): 147–179

Burkhalter Fluckiger, J., *When the World becomes Female: Guises of a South Indian Goddess*, Indiana University Press, Bloomington/Indianapolis 2013

Census of India 1961, vol. II, Andhra Pradesh, Part VII-A (1), Selected Crafts of Andhra Pradesh, ed. Chandra Sekhar, A., Manager of Publications, New Delhi 1965

Claus, P., 'Katama Raju', in Mills, M. A., Claus, P. J. and Diamond, S. (eds), *South Asian Folklore: An Encyclopedia*, Routledge, New York 2003: 329–330

Clothey, F.W., 'Pilgrimage Centres in the Tamil Cultus of Murukan', in *Journal of the American Academy of Religion* vol. XL no. 1 (March 1972): 79–95

Clothey, F.W., *The Many Faces of Murukan: The History and Meaning of a South Indian God*, Munshiram Manoharlal, New Delhi 2005

Cohen, S., 'The Unusual Textile Trade between India and Sri Lanka: Block Prints and Chintz 1550–1900', in Crill, R. (ed.), *Textiles from India: The Global Trade*, Seagull Publications, Calcutta/London/New York 2006: 56–80

Crill, R., *Chintz: Indian Textiles for the West*, V&A, London 2008

Crill, R. (ed.), *The Fabric of India*, V&A, London 2015

Dallapiccola, A.L., 'Ramayana in Southern Indian Art', in Verghese, A. and Dallapiccola, A.L. (eds), *South India Under Vijayanagara*, Oxford University Press, New Delhi 2011: 183–193

Dallapiccola, A.L., 'The Ramayana: Two 19th century Canopies from Coastal Andhra in the Victoria and Albert Museum', in Dallapiccola, A.L. (ed.), *Indian Painting: The Lesser Known Traditions,* Niyogi Books, New Delhi 2011: 138–155

Dallapiccola, A.L., *South Indian Paintings: Catalogue of the British Museum Collection*, British Museum Press, London 2010

Dallapiccola, A.L., *Dictionary of Hindu Lore and Legend*, Thames and Hudson, London 2002

Dessigane, R. and Pattabiramin, P.Z., *La Légende de Skanda selon le Kandapuranam tamoul et l'iconographie*, Institut Français d'Indologie, Pondichery 1967

Fuller, C., 'The "Holy Family" of Shiva in a South Indian temple', [online] LSE Research Online, London 1995

Gittinger, M., *Master Dyers to the World: Technique and Trade in Early Indian Dyed Cotton Textiles*, The Textile Museum, Washington DC 1982

Guy, J., *Woven Cargoes: Indian Textiles in the East*, Thames and Hudson, London 1998

Hadaway, W. S., *Cotton Painting and Printing in the Madras Presidency*, Government Press, Madras 1917

Hall, M., 'Painters on Cotton: Collection in the Victoria & Albert Museum, London', in *Homage to Kalamkari*, Marg Publications, Bombay 1979: 95–114.

Hari Rao, V.N., *The Srirangam Temple: Art and Architecture*, Sri Venkateswara University, Tirupati 1967

Harle, J.C. and Topsfield, A., *Indian Art in the Ashmolean Museum*, Ashmolean Museum, Oxford 1987

Harman, W.P., *The Sacred Marriage of a Hindu Goddess*, Indiana University Press, Bloomington/Indianapolis 1989

Hart, G.L. and Heifetz, H., *The Forest Book of the Ramayana of Kampan*, University of California Press, Berkeley/Los Angeles/London, 1988

Havell, E.B., 'The Industries of Madras', in *Journal of Indian Art and Industry* vol. III, no. 27 (1890): 10–16

Hudson, D., 'Two Citra festivals in Madurai', in Welbon, G.R. and Yocum, G.E. (eds), *Religious Festivals in South India and Sri Lanka*, Manohar, New Delhi 1982: 101–156

Irwin, J. and Brett, K.B., *Origins of Chintz*, H.M.S.O., London/Toronto 1970

Irwin, J. and Hall, M., *Indian Painted and Printed Fabrics*, vol. I, Historic Textiles at the Calico Museum, Calico Museum, Ahmedabad 1971

Jayakar, P., 'Gaiety in Colour and Form: Painted and Printed Cloths', in *Homage to Kalamkari*, Marg, Mumbai 1979: 23–34

L'Hernault, F., *L'Iconographie de Subrahmanya au Tamilnad,* Institut Français d'Indologie, Pondichery 1978

Liebert, G., *Iconographic Dictionary of the Indian Religions: Hinduism–Buddhism–Jainism*, E.J. Brill, Leiden 1976

Mani, V., *Puranic Encyclopaedia*, Motilal Banarasidass, New Delhi 1979

Michell, G., *Architecture and Art of Southern India: Vijayanagara and the Successor States*, Cambridge University Press, London 1995

Mohanty, B.C., et al, *Natural Dyeing Processes of India*, Calico Museum of Textiles, Ahmedabad 1987

Nagabhushana Sarma, M., *Folk Performing Arts of Andhra Pradesh*. Telugu University, Hyderabad 1995

Narayana Rao, V., 'Tricking the Goddess: Cowherd Katamaraju and Goddess Ganga in the Telugu Folk Epic', in Hiltebeitel, A. (ed.), *Criminal Gods and Demon Devotees: Essays on the Guardians of Popular Hinduism*, State University of New York Press, Albany 1989: 105–121

Narayana Rao, V., 'Epics and Ideologies: Six Telugu Folk Epics', in Blackburn, S. and Ramanujan, A.K. (eds), *Another Harmony: New Essays on the Folklore of India*, University of California Press, Berkeley 1986

Perera, E.W., *Sinhalese Banners and Standards*, Colombo Museum, Colombo 1916

Polo, Marco, *Il Milione*, Benedetto, L.F. (ed.), Leo S. Olschki, Firenze 1928

Richman, P. (ed.), *Many Ramayanas: The Diversity of a Narrative Tradition in South Asia*, University of California Press, Berkeley 1991

Richman, P., 'E.V. Ramasami's Reading of the Ramayana', in Richman, P. (ed.), *Many Ramayanas: The Diversity of a Narrative Tradition in South Asia*, University of California Press, Berkeley 1991: 175–201

Roghair, G.H., *The Epic of Palnadu*, Clarendon Press, Oxford 1982

Sadanandam, P., *Art and Culture of the Marginalised Nomadic Tribes in Andhra Pradesh*, Gyan Publishing House, New Delhi 2008

Sarma, C.R., *The Ramayana in Telugu and Tamil: A Comparative Study*, Lakshminarayana Granthamala, Madras 1973

Sen, S. (ed.), *Indian Travels of Thevenot and Careri, Being the third part of the travels of M de Thevenot into the Levant and the third part of a voyage round the world by Dr John Francis Gemelli Careri*, National Archives of India, New Delhi 1949

Srinivas, S., *Rajamahendri Ramayana Paintings*, Drusya Kala Deepika, Vishakapatnam 2005

Shulman, D.D., *Tamil Temple Myths, Sacrifice and Divine Marriage in the South Indian Saiva Tradition*, Princeton University Press, Princeton 1980

Smith, W.L., 'The Ramayana in Eastern India', in Bose, M. (ed.), *The Ramayana Revisited*, Oxford University Press, New York 2004: 87–106

Smith, W.L., *Ramayana Traditions in Eastern India, Assam, Bengal, Orissa*, Stockholm Studies in Indian Languages and Culture 2, Department of Indology, University of Stockholm, Stockholm 1988

Stutterheim, W., *Rama-Legends and Rama Reliefs in Indonesia*, translated from German by C.D. Paliwal and R.P. Jain, IGNCA and Abhinav Publications, New Delhi 1989

Subba Rao, T.V., 'The Ballad cycle of Katama Raju: a Telugu Folk epic', in Reddy, Ramakrishna B. (ed.), *Dravidian Folk and Tribal Lore*, Dravidian University, Kuppam 2001: 189–198

Talbot, C., *Precolonial India in Practice: Society, Region and Identity in Medieval Andhra*, Oxford University Press, New York 2001

Thangavelu, K., 'Mandecculu', in Mills, M.A., Claus, P. J. and Diamond, S. (eds), *South Asian Folklore: An Encyclopedia*, Routledge, New York 2003: 377

Thangavelu, K., 'Oral and Performative Dimensions of A Painted Scroll from Telangana', in Dallapiccola, A.L. (ed.), *Indian Painting: The Lesser Known Traditions*, Niyogi Books, New Delhi 2011: 126–137

Thangavelu, K., 'Itinerant Images: Embodiments of Art and Narrative in Telangana', in Jain, J. (ed.), *Picture Showmen: Insights into the Narrative Traditions in Indian Art*, Marg Publications, Mumbai 1998: 90–99

Thurston, E. and Rangachari, K., *Castes and Tribes of Southern India*, 7 vols [1909], Cosmo Publications, Delhi 1975

Valmiki, *The Ramayana of Valmiki*, vol. I: *Balakanda*, translated by Robert P. Goldman, Princeton University Press, Princeton 1984

Valmiki, *The Ramayana of Valmiki*, vol. II: *Ayodhyakanda*, translated by S.I. Pollock, Princeton University Press, Princeton 1986

Valmiki, *The Ramayana of Valmiki*, vol. III: *Aranyakanda*, translated by S.I. Pollock, Princeton University Press, Princeton 1991

Varadarajan, L., *South Indian Traditions of Kalamkari*, National Institute of Design, Ahmedabad 1982

Verghese, A., *Archaeology, Art and Religion: New Perspectives on Vijayanagara*, Oxford University Press, New Delhi 2000

Walker, B., *Hindu World*, 2 vols, George Allen and Unwin, London 1968

Whitehead. H., *The Village Gods of South India*, 2nd edition, revised and enlarged, Oxford University Press, London/New York 1921

Zvelebil, K.V., *Two Tamil Folk Tales: The Story of King Matanakama, The Story of Peacock Ravana*, Motilal Banarasidass and UNESCO, Delhi/Paris 1987

Websites

http://www.Srirangam.org/
http://www.Tiruchendur.org
http://www.Murugan.org/temples
http://www.YouTube.com/watch?v=rTQ0Be3dsUw
['*Alagar is Coming*', video of Alagar Koyil Festival]

Glossary

abhaya mudra gesture of reassurance in which the right hand is held upright, palm facing outwards.

abhisheka sprinkling of consecrated water over a religious image or on the head of a king at his coronation.

acharya teacher, preceptor, especially in the Sri Vaishnava religious tradition.

agni-astra 'fire weapon', a magical weapon used by Rama.

agnihotra 'fire offering', an important Vedic rite; epithet of Agni, the deity of fire.

agnikunda fire pit used in Vedic rituals.

akshate raw rice, coloured with turmeric and saffron, used during rituals, especially marriage.

alvar(s) twelve South Indian poet-saints, devotees of Vishnu (7th–9th cent. CE).

amrita nectar of immortality retrieved from the depths of the Ocean of Milk.

amrita kalasha vessel containing the nectar of immortality.

angavastra cloth worn by men on the shoulders and chest.

anjali mudra gesture of respectful greeting or adoration. Both hands are clasped together, palms touching.

annakavadi see *kavadi*.

apsara(s) dancers and courtesans of the gods.

arati temple ritual in which a flame is waved in a clockwise direction in front of the sacred image.

aruval long curved machete-like knife. Typical attribute of Karuppusvami.

asana seat, throne, posture, sitting position.

Ashokavana garden of *ashoka* trees, where Sita was held captive.

ashrama retreat of a sage, place of meditation and prayer.

ashtadikpala(s) the eight guardians of the cardinal directions: Indra, Agni, Yama, Nairruti, Varuna, Vayu, Kubera and Ishana.

ashvamedha yajna/yaga the prestigious *ashvamedha*, horse sacrifice, was a special rite for extending territory and royal power. The king and his army followed the horse; if it happened to cross over the boundary into another ruler's state, that ruler either had to submit to the invading king or establish his supremacy in battle. Eventually, on its return, the horse was ritually killed.

asura(s) rivals of the gods.

astra 'weapon'. In particular, magical weapons, e.g. *agni-astra* (fire weapon), *naga-astra* (snake-weapon).

avatara(s) 'descent', term usually applied to the ten incarnations, *dashavatara*, of Vishnu.

Battar(s) Tamil Brahmin community.

Beda(s) a community of hunters and warriors settled mainly in Karnataka, known as *Boya* in Andhra Pradesh.

bhiksha 'alms'.

bhikshu 'mendicant'.

bhuta(s) originally 'living being', the term has come to designate a group of malevolent spirits.

bijaksharam a mystic syllable which forms the essential part of a mantra.

Boya(s) a community of hunters and warriors settled mainly in Andhra Pradesh and Tamil Nadu; see also *Beda*(s).

brahma-astra a magical weapon used by Rama.

brahmotsava 'Brahma's festival', one of the most important festivals of a temple.

chakra 'discus', 'wheel'. Typical attribute of Vishnu.

chakravarti 'universal ruler', a powerful ruler whose dominion extends over the whole earth.

chamara fly-whisk generally made of yak-tail, a symbol of kingship.

chayakkontai 'bent on one side'. Typical headgear of some deities whose hair is tied in a bun on the side of the head and covered by a crown.

chidi mari 'swing festival', also known as 'hook swinging'. Ritual performed by men at the beginning of the spring in honour of a goddess (e.g. Gangamma, Mariyamman, etc.). This festival is also known as *charak puja*.

chinnamayuru a type of trumpet.

Chittirai festival the most important annual festival celebrated in Madurai during the month of *Chittirai* (April–May). It celebrates, among others, the wedding of the goddess Minakshi to Sundareshvara.

chudamani jewel worn on the hair parting and resting on the forehead.

crore ten-million.

daf tambourine.

damaru hourglass-shaped drum, around which a cobra is often coiled; typical attribute of Shiva.

danda 'rod', 'staff', typical attribute of a number of deities, e.g. Yama, Subrahmanya.

danda-astra a magical weapon used by Ravana.

dargah shrine built over the grave of a revered religious figure, often a Sufi saint or dervish.

darshana 'sight' of the deity, the crucial moment of a temple visit in which the devotee makes eye contact with the enshrined deity.

deva(s), devata(s) 'deity'.

dikpala(s) see *ashtadikpala(s)*.

dipa vriksha 'tree of lamps', a tree-shaped oil lamp used in temple rituals.

divyadesham(s) 'divine abodes'; this name refers to 108 Vishnu temples mentioned in the works of the *alvar*(s).

duppati 'blanket'.

dvarapala 'door guardian' placed at the entrance of every sacred compound or shrine.

gada 'mace', 'club'; typical attribute of Vishnu.

gandharva(s), gandharvi(s) musicians and singers of the gods.

garbha griha 'womb-house'; the essential element of a temple, the sanctuary in which the deity is enshrined.

ghanta 'bell'.

ghee clarified butter.

Golla(s) important pastoral community settled mainly in Andhra Pradesh and Telangana, also known as *Yadava*.

gopa(s) cowherd.

gopi(s), gopika(s) the milkmaids in love with Krishna.

gopura towered gateway leading from the street into

a temple complex, typical of South Indian temples.

grantha this term may either refer to the script used for writing Sanskrit texts in South India, or may designate any sacred text.

hamsa 'goose'; vehicle of Brahma.

hamsa-vahana 'goose vehicle' used in temple processions to carry the metal images of the deities.

Jangalu(s) Virashaiva minstrel priest.

jata(s) knot of matted hair worn by ascetics, and characteristic of Shiva.

jatamakuta, jatamudi 'crown of matted hair', headdress, often with ornaments; characteristic of many forms of Shiva.

jatra festival, pilgrimage. Also, *yatra*.

kalasha 'water pot', an auspicious symbol; *kalasha*-shaped architectural elements crown the top of sacred buildings.

Kallar(s) A warrior community settled in the Madurai district.

Kalpavriksha 'wishing tree', one of the five trees of the gods which grant every wish.

Kamadhenu 'wish(-fulfilling) cow'. The mythical cow of plenty who can grant any wish to her owner.

kamandalu water vessel generally used by ascetics, typical attribute of several deities, e.g. Brahma.

kapala 'cup, alms-bowl of a beggar, skull (-cup)'. Cup made from the upper part of a human cranium, a typical attribute of Shaiva deities.

karnapattra(s) 'ear-leaf', large ornaments which cover the ears of an image.

kavadi 'yoke'. A semi-circular decorated canopy supported by a wooden rod carried to the temple on the shoulders of the devotee. **Annakavadi**, a *kavadi* bearing two containers which are used to carry food, especially rice and milk.

kinnara(s), kinnari(s) 'what (kind of a) man?', semi divine beings characterized by human faces and birds' bodies with foliated tails. *Kinnara*(s) and *gandharva*(s) are the heavenly musicians of the gods.

kirttimukha 'face of glory', decorative motif in the shape of a lion mask, frequently used at the top of an arch, and often seen in stone and metal sculpture.

kodanda 'bow', typical attribute of Rama.

kodimaram flagstaff.

Komati(s) South Indian trading community.

Kommulavaru, Kommulavallu a community of folk singers in Andhra Pradesh and Telangana. Their name derives from the brass horn-shaped wind instrument, *kommu*, they play in their performances.

koyil 'temple'.

kudumi knot of hair tied at the back of the head, often worn by Brahmins.

kulayi tall conical cap which came into fashion in the mid-15th century and continued to be a popular headdress in the subsequent centuries.

lagnam 'ascendant', the sign of the zodiac on the eastern horizon at the time of a person's birth.

lalitasana 'posture of relaxation' in which the left leg is usually resting upon the seat while the right leg hangs down along it.

latasundari 'beauty (clutching a) creeper', an auspicious motif frequently depicted in painting and sculpture.

linga 'sign', 'gender', 'sex'; an iconic form of Shiva, a symbol of the male principle.

lota 'water bottle', small round metal pot.

lungi garment wound around the waist and tucked in at the front.

maddalam drum which is hung around the waist of the player.

maddale barrel-shaped drum, typical of Karnataka.

makara mythical aquatic creature with scrolls issuing from its mouth, frequently used as a decorative motif.

makuta 'crown', 'diadem', 'tiara'.

mala 'garland'; flower garland, chaplet.

mandapa columned hall; **mayil mandapa** (peacock *mandapa*); **vrishabha mandapa**; **Nandi mandapa** (bull *mandapa*).

mantra 'magic formula', 'mystical syllable(s)'.

matha religious centre, often combined with a school.

mayil mandapa see *mandapa*.

mudra 'seal', 'sign', 'token'. Gesture with a specific esoteric meaning.

muhurta the thirtieth part of a day, i.e. 48 minutes.

mukhalinga type of *linga* on which one or more faces representing different aspects of Shiva are carved.

muni 'sage', 'seer', an ascetic, especially one who has taken a vow of silence.

murti 'form', 'likeness, statue'; images depicting the different aspects of the deities.

naga-astra 'snake-weapon'; one of the many magical weapons mentioned in the epics.

nagakannika(s) 'snake girls', e.g. the wives of the snake Kalinga.

nagapasha 'snake-noose', magical weapon typical of Indrajit.

nagara large drum played with sticks.

nagasvaram wind instrument similar to the *shenai* of North India but larger.

naivedyam food offered to the deities.

namam mark drawn on the forehead with coloured earth, sandalwood or ash.

natha(s) follower of a sect of Shaivas who practise extreme forms of asceticism.

navagunjara a creature composed of nine different animals: it has the head of a rooster, and stands on three feet: those of an elephant, tiger and deer or horse. The fourth limb is a raised human arm carrying a lotus or a wheel. It has the neck of a peacock, the back or hump of a bull, the waist of a lion, and the tail is of a serpent.

olai leaf of the palmyra palm used for manuscripts.

pachisi a board game.

pada puja see *puja*.

palampore a type of hand-painted and mordant dyed bed cover that was made in India for the export market during the 18th century and very early 19th century.

pallivasal mosque.

pan, pan–supari preparation of betel (*pan*) leaf and areca nut (*supari*); it is offered to a sacred image as a form of worship; in private homes the offering of *pan–supari* to a guest at the end of a meal is a standard form of hospitality.

pankha large swinging fan, fixed to the ceiling, and pulled by a servant.

parashu 'axe', characteristic attribute of several deities, e.g. Parashurama.

parijata (*Nyctanthes arbor tristis*) Indian coral tree, a mythical tree which emerged from the Churning of the Milk Ocean.

pasha 'noose', characteristic attribute of deities such as Yama and of Varuna, guardians respectively of the southern and of the western directions.

payasa a sweet, preparation of milk and pulses.

picchwai(s) painted hangings illustrating various aspects of Krishna as Sri Nathji, produced at Nathdwara in Rajasthan.

pinda 'lump', 'ball' of boiled rice, sesame seed, honey and butter.

pitha, pithakam 'seat'; in iconography, the pedestal of an image.

prakara 'bounding wall'; the walled precinct of a temple, especially in the case of concentric enclosures.

puja 'offering', 'worship', 'homage' before a sacred image. **Pada puja** 'worship of the feet' of a deity, or of a spiritual teacher.

puja namaskaram a ritual to ensure the smooth running of any undertaking.

pujari priest who performs the *puja*.

Purana(s) 'ancient', 'old'; a literary genre dealing with ancient tales and legends, old traditional history.

Pushpaka Vimana 'flower chariot'; the aerial conveyance on which Rama and his allies returned to Ayodhya.

pushpavarsha 'rain of flowers'; a way of honouring deities and heroes by letting flowers and flower petals fall on them.

putrakameshti yajna/yaga a complex sacrifice to ensure the birth of a son.

rahukala 'Rahu time'; an inauspicious time occurring daily at different hours.

rakshasa(s) goblins, evil spirits.

rishi sage, seer, inspired poet.

rudraksha (*Elaeocarpus sphericus*) its dried seeds are used in particular by Shaivas to make beads for their rosaries.

sadhu a renouncer; one who has attained (supernatural) powers.

Sanjivi Parvata a mountain on which grow medicinal plants.

sannyasi one who has renounced the world for a life of solitude.

Saptarishi(s) 'the seven rishis', the legendary founders of the orthodox Brahmin lineages.

shakti 'energy', 'divine power'. Personification of the female divine power; the energy of any deity.

shakti 'spear', 'lance'; characteristic attribute of Subrahmanya. See also *vel*.

shankha 'conch'; characteristic attribute of Vishnu. As a musical instrument, *shankhu*, the conch is used in temples, religious ceremonies and processions.

shatari a silver crown on which the feet of Vishnu are embossed, placed briefly on the head of each devotee by the *pujari* at the end of the *puja*.

shenai a wind instrument whose sound is thought to create and maintain a sense of auspiciousness and sanctity. It is the North Indian counterpart of the *nagasvaram*.

stambha 'column'; erected opposite a sanctuary, bearing the image of the *vahana* and enshrined deity, e.g. Garuda *stambha* in Vaishnava temples.

stupi vase finial, topmost part of a temple's superstructure.

stupika small dome-like structure crowning the top of the roof in South Indian temples.

sumangali(s) a woman whose husband is alive, whose presence is deemed auspicious at weddings and other religious ceremonies.

svarga 'world of light'; the abode of the gods.

svami 'master'; used also to refer to a deity.

tala(s) cymbals.

taluka administrative subdivision of a district.

tanka 'chisel', 'axe'; typical attribute of Subrahmanya.

tarai a type of trumpet.

tavula a type of drum.

tilaka 'round mark on the forehead'; the caste mark.

tirtha 'bathing place', 'passage'. Shrine or sacred bathing place; place of pilgrimage.

tripundra three horizontal marks worn on the forehead by the devotees of Shiva.

trishula trident; characteristic attribute of Shiva, Devi and several other deities.

utsavamurti, utsvabera processional image, generally bronze, of a deity dressed and decorated, brought from the temple on festival occasions.

vahana 'vehicle'. The conveyance of a deity, often an animal.

vajra 'thunderbolt'; characteristic attribute of various deities, e.g. Indra.

vanara(s) 'denizen of the forest', i.e. monkeys, allies of Rama.

varada mudra hand position indicating the granting of a wish. The left hand is held out palm uppermost, with fingers pointing downwards.

vata (*Ficus benghalensis*) banyan tree. **Vatapatra**: leaf of the banyan tree on which Krishna reclines while floating on the primeval waters.

vayu-astra 'wind weapon'; one of the many magical weapons mentioned in the epics.

vel 'spear'; typical attribute of Subrahmanya. See also *shakti*.

venu 'flute'; characteristic attribute of Krishna as Venugopala, the 'cowherd with the flute'.

vina stringed instrument of many different types; characteristic attribute of Narada, Sarasvati and other deities.

Virashaiva(s) or Lingayats, followers of Shiva; a South Indian religious group.

vrishabha mandapa, see *mandapa*.

Yadava(s) see *Golla(s)*.

yaga, yajna 'oblation', 'offering', 'sacrifice'.

yagashala, yajnashala 'offering or sacrifice hall'.

yajnopavita 'sacred thread', worn by the three 'upper castes' of Hindu society, slung over the left shoulder and hanging down under the right arm.

yali leogryph, mythical lion-faced animal.

yatra see *jatra*.

yojana a distance of about ten miles.

yuddha 'battle'.

zamindar 'land owner'.

Acknowledgements

My interest in the V&A collection of painted textiles dates back to July 1990 when I had a fleeting glimpse of some of them. At that time the Students Room was being re-structured, and practically off limits. It was through the kind permission of Dr. Deborah Swallow, then Keeper of the Indian Department that I was permitted to have a look to this material for the first time. Nothing had prepared me for the world of colour and exuberant design, which were briefly displayed; immediately the idea of studying them crossed my mind.

About eighteen years later, this idea came to fruition thanks to Rosemary Crill, Senior Curator (South Asia) in the Asian Department, who from the very inception of this project has always been welcoming and constantly helpful. Without her steady encouragement, this project would not have been possible. I would also like to thank the staff of the Asian Department, in particular Nick Barnard and Divia Patel, who were always generous with their time, and ready at hand when help was needed especially in handling the large, unwieldy textiles.

This study could not have been attempted without the crucial help of Dr. (Mrs.) Mangalam Mathrubutham, who read and translated all the Telugu and Tamil captions on the textiles. Her intimate local knowledge, her patience and her sense of humour have been a great and continuous support throughout the years.

I am greatly indebted to Dr. Steven Cohen for his valuable comments in the drafting of parts of the text. T. Richard Blurton has facilitated my access to the British Museum collections and has been, as always, a steady encouragement throughout the years. A special thanks goes to Prof. Indira V. Peterson, Mount Holyoke College, USA, for kindly taking the time to discuss with me some parts of this project.

In order to try to decode the intricate story of Katamaraju (cat. 12 and cat. 13), presented here for the first time, I relied on the help of a number of colleagues whose special expertise is folklore: Dr. S. Charsley, Dr. P. Sadanandam, Dr. P. Subbachary and Dr. K. Thangavelu, to all of whom I am deeply indebted.

I also thank Bipin Shah and his team at Mapin Publishing, Ahmedabad and Mark Eastment and V&A Publishing, who have supported this project from an early date.

Anna L. Dallapiccola